Good Work Good Business

Good Work Good Business

Practical People Strategies for a Changing World

Authors:

Michelle Bailey	Siân Perham
Shirley Borrett	Marc Reid
Julie Huish	Sally Stiegler
Marjory Mair	Julie Taylor
Adrian Marsh	Adrian Wheatley
Heather Mills	

Copyright © 2020 by the authors listed above.

3

Good Work Good Business

Table of Contents

Foreword

A year ago we ran an amazing one day workshop where a group of ten experienced HR professionals produced a 'Book in a Day'. It was a project that resulted from an idea we had whilst running the local CIPD Special Interest Group for HR Consultants. The thinking was to bring together a group who could all write a chapter each and use Amazon's Kindle Direct Publishing system to publish the book during the one day workshop. It worked, and a year ago we published '*The Future of Work. Practical People Strategies for Business Leaders*' both in eBook and paperback form.

The event was so successful that there was sufficient interest to run it again in 2020. But as we all know, 2020 did not turn out as planned! So this years book has taken a different route to production. Whilst we have kept the workshop where we produce and publish the book in real time during the day, it has all been done online using the power of Zoom. We have also taken the opportunity provided by remote working to have catch up sessions in the lead up to the workshop so we could share our chapter drafts and receive feedback. This has been a valuable addition to our process and we trust that the resulting book has benefitted accordingly both in content and format quality.

We are very grateful to the outstanding group of talented HR and people professionals who have contributed to this book. The group brings together many years of experience and knowledge from across the people related work spectrum, including expertise in leadership, change management, work culture, career management, remote learning, conflict management, generalist HR, employment law and employee engagement. Each of the chapter authors has brought their own specialist insight to focus on a particular aspect of the overall theme of Good Work Good Business, set against the context of a changing world. A key aim has been to keep the chapters accessible and practical, offering valuable tools and strategies that business leaders can apply in their own workplaces.

We also appreciate the support of the CIPD and in particular Dr Wilson Wong, Head of Insight and Futures at the CIPD who has lent his great expertise to our project by writing the Introduction and participating in the workshop. We are also indebted to Jo Hutchinson who has given us the benefit of her vast experience in the world of publishing to help us improve our writing.

We hope you enjoy this book and find some nuggets within it which will help you with the challenging business of managing people. Through buying the book you are not only helping yourself and the people you manage but also you are supporting the charity Trussell Trust Stop UK Hunger as all proceeds from this book will be donated to this worthy cause.

Michelle Bailey and Marc Reid

August 2020

Introduction

"Management is doing things right; leadership is doing the right things."

— Peter Drucker, Management consultant

The year 2020 will be remembered for generations. There will be films, books and lots of research papers and theses on the minutiae of what happened, blame apportioned and unsung heroes revealed. I applaud the spirit of the CIPD Thames Valley consultant community in responding so creatively and productively in a time of crisis.

The chapters reflect a wealth of life experience and professional practice and a generosity of heart. I look forward to reading all the chapters to learn, and to share that learning in turn.

Following from Drucker, the chapters here aim to help you to do things right, which is no mean feat. How do you do things right when #metoo and #BlackLivesMatter show up areas of myopia and fear in your organization? How do you continue to draw together a dispersed workforce, many fearful that they may not be secure. There are chapters here on Culture Change, Change Programmes and Workplace conflict, and the centrality of trust in the employment relationship. Doing things right is part of being a professional, of lifelong (re)discovery, a beagle in search of the better game.

But this project is also about doing the right things and this book aims to inspire and equip you to make a difference in improving the working lives of the many people you lead and manage. CIPD has been championing good work since its origins as the Welfare Workers' Association in 1913. To that end, we've has spent years developing a CIPD Good Work Index (GWI) which has distilled 7 key dimensions and their interactions:

- Pay and benefits
- The contractual relationship
- Work–life balance and flexible working (even more salient in the pandemic era)
- Job design and the how work life is organised/ experienced
- Relationships at work including the quality of people management
- Employee voice
- Health and wellbeing

CIPD believes that Good work should be accessible to all, regardless of personal characteristics or occupation, and that the people profession plays a leading role in ensuring that work is both productive for the organisation and good for employees. The CIPD GWI gives insights that help individuals, employers and policy makers improve and protect job quality at every level.

CIPD also actively develops British and International Standards in people management and development in support of Good work. *BS76000 HR - Valuing people – Management system -Requirements and guidance* enshrines the key principles for organizations who want to set themselves apart as good employers. The first principle – 'People working on behalf of the organization have intrinsic value in addition to their protections under the law or in regulation, which needs to be respected' – gives you some idea of the scope of the BS76000 family of standards which include *BS76005* on Diversity and Inclusion, *PD76006* Learning and Development, and *PAS3002* and *ISO45001* for health, safety and wellbeing. There's a succinct introduction in the CIPD factsheet HR and Standards.

The British Social Attitudes Survey (2016), showed that between 1989 and 2015 the share of good jobs, as defined by the researchers increased, and that it was the young and the 'working class' who benefited most. But the BSAS also identified significant groups who lost out, like older workers in more routine jobs. The same survey also suggested little overall improvement in job security between 2005 and 2015, with again some groups experiencing a marked decline, and increased reporting of stress.

So, while the overall position has improved over the past 20 years, there is evidence of greater polarisation between the majority and a significant minority for whom work has become worse. As this pandemic year has revealed, there are many workers forgotten and much more to be done. #HRTogether has shown what a force the people profession is when focused. Let us use this crisis to reset our expectations of what is normal in the employment relationship and bring about better work and productive working lives to the many.

Dr Wilson Wong
Head of Insight & Futures, CIPD
Indept Chair Human Capital Standards & Deputy Chair
Knowledge Management Committees, BSI
Visiting Professor Nottingham Business School.

19 August 2020

About the Author

Adrian Wheatley

www.adrianwheatley.co.uk

Before setting up on his own, Adrian spent a busy career across a variety of industry sectors in both large and small organisations. He has worked with leaders as coach and facilitator in strategic, operational and international contexts.

He is a Member of the Chartered Institute of Personnel and Development, holds an MA in Human Resource Management and a Diploma in Management Coaching & Mentoring.

His chapter "Developing Teams for the Future – is it still relevant?" appeared in "The Future of Work" (ISBN 9781072658955) published in 2019.

Adrian likes to divide his social time between sailing and spending time in Spain where he has family. He still hasn't got it all worked it out...

Working out how to lead – practical tips from an accidental leader

By Adrian Wheatley

Introduction

When I was growing up I never thought I'd end up being responsible for leading others. This unplanned, 'accidental' move came without a conversion course and with no software upgrade of the skills and knowledge required to be an effective leader. There was plenty of written material and training on leadership available but what was I going to *do* to be effective?

At that time, the only reference points I had were what it felt like to be an employee and how managers had influenced my experience at work, good and bad. I set off trying to copy the good bits, avoid the bad and find ways to respond to the day-to-day tests that first-time managers come up against.

Over the years there have been a few courses, some academic study and I now make part of my living by delivering leadership development workshops to middle and senior managers.

When I look back, I realise that I've picked up a collection of 'nuggets' which worked for me and the teams I have led. I don't remember exactly where some of them came from, but they have served me well in leading good work and delivering good business outcomes.

The intention of this chapter is to offer some of these nuggets as tips and suggestions for practical application. I don't expect all of them to work for everyone but hope that each reader will find something which enables them to become a more effective leader (and save themselves and their teams some pain).

The world of work changed considerably when I took the plunge as a leader. This list of practical people strategies is something I wish someone had shared with me as I stumbled into that first leadership position.

 **Tip 1** Expect to be judged – you're a celebrity now

How quickly have you made

judgements about the leaders in your life? In my experience every leader (politician, executive, manager or team leader) is observed, talked about, and has opinions formed about them by those looking on. As soon as you become the leader you should expect that people will be watching you and making their minds up about whether you're worthy of the position based on such things as what they see you do, your body language, your mood, the sorts of questions you ask and what others say about you..

It seems to me that whilst you can't stop this scrutiny you can influence how you are judged by choosing how you behave. The following might help:

- Do – clearly outline the results and behaviours you are expecting
- Do – state your intentions as the leader and make sure your actions match
- Do – prepare to be unpopular sometimes
- Don't – underestimate what can be inferred from your behaviour (we've all done it...)
- Don't – try to talk your way out of something you've acted your way into
- Don't - avoid the difficult conversations – you'll be judged by what you walk past too

Tip 2 Work out who you are – understand the hard-wiring

It was quite late in life that I first started to understand the 'hard-wiring' of my personality. It started with a Myers Briggs Type Indicator report which really opened my eyes to different personality types. The report reinforced a few things I was already aware of, clarified some areas I was struggling with and helped me to recognise a few blind spots. It transformed how I looked at my own behaviour and how I could modify it to improve the effectiveness of my own style and its impact on others.

I remember wondering why this sort of thing wasn't taught at school many years earlier. Surely the ability to build effective relationships and act authentically (rather than trying to be someone else) are critical human skills and not just for leaders?

Possible strategies to deepen your understanding of who you are:

- Consider using one (or more) of the reputable psychometric tools (e.g. MBTI, DiSC) to give you a description of your personality. Recognising that your personality is unique and impossible to classify completely, does the report offer any new insights?
- Seek to understand how your personality informs your motivations and your personal values (or vice versa). What are the things that you stand for and that are non-negotiable for you?
- Ask for feedback from others to better understand your impact on them:

o   Build feedback mechanisms into your day-to-day activities. An easy way of asking for feedback is the WWW/EBI model (ask "what went well?" and seek suggestions how it could be "even better if...")

o   Use a suitable 360-degree questionnaire to give you data from several perspectives

If you can deepen your understanding of what helps and hinders you as a leader you can turn this into practical strategies to help you improve. Employing a trusted colleague or mentor/coach could help. How can you make the most of the personality you have rather than trying to be someone else?

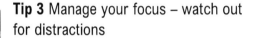 **Tip 3** Manage your focus – watch out for distractions

Your responsibilities are likely to change dramatically as you step into the leader role; planning horizons will become longer, you'll have accountability for budgets, talent management, team dynamics, risk assessment and so on.

As well as learning this new stuff, you'll still have to deliver what's required today, maybe through others, and you'll still have to make sure you're looking after yourself (see Tip 6).

It can be bewildering. I found John Adair's Action Centred Leadership model a great help in understanding, and finding balance between, three key focus areas (task, team, individual) of the leadership role.

As you grapple with juggling the various responsibilities, watch out for Monkeys and Pigs. I doubt that everyone will like these metaphors, but I offer them because they stuck with me and helped me to remain focussed. In any event, no animals were hurt during the writing of this chapter.

 Monkeys – a metaphor for problems – imagine a squirming monkey that someone has just presented to you unexpectedly. You have three choices:
- o Kill it – fix the problem quickly, or
- o Feed it – let the problem get bigger and more attached to you, or
- o Pass it on – delegate the problem to someone else.

In the interests of managing your time, try to avoid feeding and picking up other people's monkeys inadvertently (how many times have you stopped for a chat with someone in a corridor and walked away with a new problem to solve)?

 Pigs – a metaphor for the people who demand the most of your time for the least payback - the people who seem to moan about everything - the 'mood-hoovers' who hold others accountable for all their woes and bring others down with their attitude. (Make sure the behaviour is not caused by a health or wellbeing issue. These will need a different response to the one below).

To avoid getting drawn into unwinnable battles with those who choose this sort of negativity, and bearing in mind that we are all adults, I remember the saying:

> "don't fight with pigs – you both get covered in mud, but the pig loves it".

It might prove more effective for you, and the whole team, if you invest your time on the people who add value.

 ### Tip 4 Add value - no matter what you do

A great boss once advised me to "always trade in the currency of the business" when making proposals and plans so that they were relevant and in context. How could I ensure that the link to what the organisation was trying to achieve was clear and easy to see?

I've since found this advice invaluable in self-employment, but it applies to corporate life too. Ask yourself; if you were an internal consultant selling your service to the organisation, would the organisation buy it, and would it represent value for money?

Take time to ensure that your work is in context and relevant. Your job title or position on the organisation chart are unlikely to be enough to give you real influence.

Tip 5 Get into their shoes – see how it feels

It's quite likely that even though you are a leader you will still experience your organisation from the standpoint of an employee. You're likely to be making judgements about your 'celebrities' as outlined in Tip 1 above. What do they do and say that affects your working life in positive and negative ways?

I have in the past chosen to dis-engage and not do my best work for leaders who, for example, focus only on their personal success, who take the credit for my ideas and who are disinterested in my motivations for being there.

On the basis that there can be no leadership without followership, the following might help you engage with the people in your team so that they will follow you:

- Catch people doing things right - make sure you tell them when they do great work rather than speaking up only when things go wrong. The WWW/EBI model referred to in Tip 2 above is great for giving (as well as receiving) feedback. It's easy to use so you can start today!

- Give people a good listening to – this is a high priority for me in any new role and applies to customers and peers as well as team members. Ask the following three questions as a minimum:
  - o what do you do here?
  - o how can I help?
  - o what do you want out of this personally?

  These conversations will help you to judge how much you'll need to challenge and how much you'll need to support each individual and enable you to set objectives and deliver feedback in a tailored way to fit their needs.

Tip 6 Look after yourself – keep the machine well maintained

Leadership can be a hugely rewarding experience despite not always being easy. Like any machine, regular maintenance should help you to make sure that you're up to the challenges when they come. Ignore maintenance at your peril...

There is no single maintenance regime that will suit everyone so my encouragement is to consider the following to start with and decide whether they can help you to stay 'match fit' as a leader:

- Wellbeing – your physical and mental wellbeing can be maintained in many ways: exercise, diet, mindfulness, social activities etc. Assess where you are today and work out how you can remain in condition to lead the team. Consider reading up on wellbeing, access any resources within your organisation or consider finding a coach to help you

- Resilience – the analogy here is the aircraft seatbelt – making sure your own seatbelt is fastened first before helping others. You can find a resilience questionnaire on the internet as a starting point to understanding this issue. Find ways to build your own resilience so that you can serve the team well as the leader, especially during the difficult times

As an accidental leader, I was surprised to find that being in charge could sometimes be a lonely existence. At more senior levels, the number of peers often becomes fewer and, you might find, more competitive. It felt like I should know how to do everything and that asking for help might be seen as a weakness.

I recommend finding a mentor who understands this dynamic to give you a safe place to bounce ideas around and decide between a range of options for action. A great mentor to me is the person who stretches my thinking and asks the questions which no-one else is asking such as "what's the worst than can happen?" and "what do you want to do when you grow up?"

Summary – Is it worth it?

It seems to me that leadership is a bit like surfing; you have to work hard paddling against the waves, constantly looking for the next opportunity. Now and again you'll catch a wave and reap the benefits of your efforts as you surf along with the wind in your hair and sun on your back. Remember that the wave won't last for ever. Things will change, you'll lose the energy somehow, or fall off, and then it's time to turn and start paddling out again hoping it'll be even better next time...

So why go through all of this? Why take on the role of the leader? If possible, make a conscious decision to take on a leadership role rather than find yourself there by accident like I did.

In any event, the tips in this chapter and the questions in the Appendix might help you to work out what to do but, to stand any chance of success, be sure that you really want all that comes with the responsibility, good and bad.

My accident turned out to be a happy one. It was often challenging and hard work, but the times spent 'on the wave' were exhilarating. I enjoyed the feeling of making a difference and especially the joy of supporting people in the team to grow and realise their ambitions.

If my experience is anything to go by, you'll sometimes have to dig deep and find the energy and resilience to regroup and adapt but find that the rewards make it all worthwhile. Find a way to weave 'work' and 'life' together to suit you and your loved ones, keep learning, have fun, and keep an eye on what lies beyond your working life... it'll happen one day!

I hope that this chapter will help you in some way, however small. Do let me know!

APPENDIX

Questions to ask yourself as a leader

- How would I describe my leadership style to a new team?
- What are my personal values and how do they impact my motivation?
- How do I divide my time and energy between task, team and individual activities?
- How does my leadership add value to what the organisation is trying to achieve?
- What is it like to be in my team?
- What is it like to work with me as a peer?
- How much do I understand my team members' personal motivations?
- What are my support mechanisms and who is helping me to challenge my thinking?
- What would be my perfect work/life balance and how do I get there?

About the author

Adrian Marsh

www.personalcareermanagement.com

Adrian is a career coach with an MA in Career Development & Coaching Studies from Warwick University, a Registered Professional Member of the Career Development Institute, and Regional Director at Personal Career Management – the UK's leading provider of outplacement services, career coaching programmes and executive coaching for individual and corporate clients.

Prior to becoming a career coach, Adrian worked in the technology sector – a former COO with extensive international management experience spanning technical, marketing, sales, operations, strategic planning and GM roles.

He combines his personal experience of senior management with his style as a coach – encouraging career management and executive coaching clients to gain confidence, develop greater self-awareness, achieve clarity of thinking, understand their own management and career goals, better handle conflict and stress, and maximise personal effectiveness.

Whose Career Is It Anyway?

Why placing career management at the centre of a new psychological contract could be a winning strategy for organisations in the 2020s

Adrian Marsh

How is your relationship?

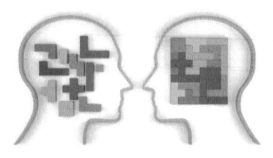

Remember the psychological contract[1]? It was a particularly hot topic in the 1980s and 1990s when many argued that the unwritten set of expectations between organisations and their workforce had been "broken" by employers. Increasing

---

[1] Hiltrop, J.M. (1995). The changing psychological contract: The human resource challenge of the 1990s. European Management Journal, 13(3)

globalisation, use of new technology and deregulation of markets had all combined to increase competition. Employers responded by delayering, outsourcing, rightsizing and making more use of contractors as they strived to become leaner and create a more flexible workforce. The old idea of a secure "job for life" in exchange for hard-work and loyalty quickly seemed like a relic from a bygone age for many workers. Wind forward twenty years and the trends have continued to the extent that in some sectors a sense of chronic job insecurity prevails.

Flexibility is clearly an advantage for organisations, but perhaps there is also a downside to a much looser psychological contract. A Gallup poll of US businesses in 2014[2] found that less than a third of US workers were actively engaged in their work, the rest being either not engaged (> 50%) or actively disengaged, with Millennials the least engaged demographic. Why do disengaged workers stay in jobs they are not enjoying? The answer may be fear – in a major survey conducted by the CIPD in 2018[3], 46% of employees said they disagreed with the statement that "they could find another job with similar conditions easily". Disengaged employees sticking in jobs solely because they doubt their prospects outside are unlikely to be performing at their best. One tech sector CEO of my acquaintance privately admitted what they wanted to see instead was "happy leavers".

---

[2] https://news.gallup.com/poll/181289/majority-employees-not-engaged-despite-gains-2014.aspx

[3] https://www.cipd.co.uk/Images/UK-working-lives-2_tcm18-40225.pdf

Employers rightly devote significant time and attention to boosting employee

> "What I'd like to see is happy leavers"
>
> **Tech Sector CEO**

engagement; but perhaps revisiting the psychological contract and boosting employees' confidence about their career prospects may be a way of getting towards an important root cause of disengagement. Is there a way to "upgrade" the psychological contract to meet the needs of the 2020s and find a better solution that is workable for employers, viable in a fiercely competitive globalised economic environment and still boosts employees' career confidence?

This chapter explores these questions and investigates what organisations can do to forge a new type of strong and healthy psychological contract with their employees – one which reflects the realities of careers today. It highlights a range of approaches that organisations can take to boost career development opportunities, and to equip their employees with the skills required to manage their career within their current organisation and beyond. It argues that such a system, by tapping into employees' natural sources of motivation, can offer significant benefits for both organisations and their employees. I have dubbed this approach **Boundaryless Career Management** and explore how it can be implemented towards the end of this chapter.

First though, let us take a step back and ask some searching questions.

Why do People Work?

 Ask someone why they work, and (especially after a tough day) they may answer "to pay the bills". Although a trite response, when finances are tight, that is indeed a pressing reason for people to work. But once a certain level of stability and social status have been secured, it truly seems as though people are looking for something more. As far back as the 1940s, Abraham Mazlow[4] gave this striving for something more the mysterious-sounding label of "self-actualization"; describing a whole string of factors that can contribute to achieving fulfilment, including autonomy, purpose, creativity, and fairness. More recently, Daniel Pink[5] has described a simplified set of these factors, identifying Autonomy, Mastery and Purpose as the keys to motivation, with the unexpected finding that financial rewards can sometimes have a negative impact on performance.

Whilst not proposing for a second that reducing salary is likely to boost motivation, nor that employees will not give the impression to their manager that achieving their next pay rise is all-important, I *am* often struck in my work as a career coach at how unimportant factors such as salary or promotion are for many clients. Indeed, it frequently takes a prompt from me before some clients consider any financial

---

[4] Reider, N. (1945). A Theory of Human Motivation: AH Maslow, Psychological Rev., L, 1943, pp. 370 396. Psychoanalytic Quarterly, 14, pp.144-145.
[5] Pink, D. H. (2009). Drive: the surprising truth about what motivates us

factors at all. An additional factor that others have sometimes added to Pink's model is the importance of well-being - a sense of psychological safety.

Another useful way of looking at self-actualization is the Japanese concept of Ikigai[6], which can be roughly translated as Purpose of Life – to be found as a result of getting the balance right between four key factors; What the World Needs, What you are Good At, What You Love and What you Can be Paid For.

---

[6] García, H., Miralles, F., & Cleary, H. (2017). Ikigai: the Japanese secret to a long and happy life.

Whose Career is it Anyway?

 Just as the employment landscape has radically changed in recent years, so new thinking has emerged about careers. Ask someone in the street what they think about when they hear the word career, and they may talk about climbing the ladder, landing a promotion, being given a pay rise etc. These ideas stem from the more stable employment landscape of the past, within which a stable multi-layered hierarchy existed and those at the top had a powerful influence on the career progression of those on the lower rungs. Although examples of such traditional careers can still be found, the economic changes already described make it less likely that this model of steady progression over time within a single organisation will be the norm, and new theories have emerged which aim to better reflect the nature of contemporary careers.

Prominent amongst these new ideas have been two related theories; Douglas Hall's idea of the Protean Career[7] and Michael Arthur's description of the Boundaryless Career[8]. These two works, seen as radical at the time of their publication have come to be accepted by many as representing the reality of contemporary careers and have

---

[7] Hall, D.T. (1996). Protean careers of the 21st century. Academy of Management Perspectives, 10(4), pp.8-16.
[8] Arthur, M.B. (1994). The boundaryless career: A new perspective for organizational inquiry. Journal of Organizational Behavior, pp.295-306.

spawned a whole new body of career research carried out of the last thirty years. The table below highlights some of the main shifts in thinking between the traditional or organisational view of careers and these new perspectives of contemporary careers.

Aspect	Traditional Careers	Contemporary Careers
ENVIRONMENT	Stable	Rapidly Changing
CAREER CHOICE	Once, at early career stage	Series of decisions at different stages
MAIN RESPONSIBILITY FOR CAREER PLANNING & MANAGEMENT	Organisation	Individual
SUCCESS MEANS	Progress through the organisational hierarchy	Psychological Success - inner feeling of achievement
CAREER HORIZON (WORKPLACE)	Within a Single Organisation	Within & External to Several Organisations
CAREER HORIZON (TIMEFRAME)	Long	Short
PROGRESS CRITERIA	Advance according to tenure	Advance according to competence & performance
LEARNING & DEVELOPMENT	Formal programmes, generalist	On-the-job, company specific, often ad-hoc

One of the most interesting findings is that as job mobility and the pace of change have increased, the main responsibility for career management has shifted from the organisation to the individual, begging the question as to how well-equipped workers are to manage their own careers.

What skills do individuals need to take control of their careers?

For many people, their career journey feels as though it has been shaped through a complex interaction of many factors, external events and chance happenings: their own skills and interests naturally, but also how their parents earnt their living, the influence of certain teachers, subject options chosen, a chance comment or suggestion made at a key moment, impressions picked up from the media, grades achieved, courses they were accepted for, contacts made... all leading up to the first "real" job they landed.

The largely unplanned nature of careers often continues from there too – people progress to a second job because they were qualified from the first, there were cities they wanted to live in, chance meetings or events happened, relationships and children had a huge impact on their lives, there were managers they got on particularly well or badly with, external economic factors impinged on their working lives, and so it continues. Despite this complex web, there are ways in which individuals can take the reins and be more pro-active about managing their careers.

Research suggests there are two "meta-competencies" critical for successful career management – **Self Awareness** and **Adaptability**[9]. Master these two, and individuals should be equipped to develop the other career management skills they will need along the way.

Whilst at first glance it may seem these are natural aptitudes, for most, developing either to the level required for successful career management requires time, effort, support, and training. Attaining self-awareness requires insight, input from others and opportunity for reflection. Career adaptability goes way beyond simply being flexible and taking whatever comes, it also encompasses planning; building on self-awareness to see what changes are required to achieve our career goals.

What impact does the changing career landscape have on organisations?

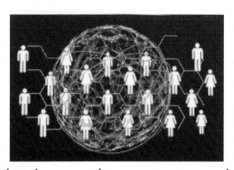 If all this change in the employment landscape is a big adjustment for individuals, so it is for organisations too. We have already touched on the battle for employee engagement, but there are other concerns too, such as understanding and

---

[9] Larios, 2013. International conference: Life design and career counseling: Building hope and resilience. Padova, Italy.

addressing the career priorities in a multi-generational workforce, attracting the best new talent into the organisation and retaining key workers.

Career priorities within a multi-generational workforce

Many recent studies[10] have investigated attitudes to work amongst Baby Boomers, Gen X, Millennials and Gen Y workers. A common finding is that alignment with the organisations values and principles are a more important factor for Millennials than older workers, but overall research suggests that the differences are not that great. One thing is clear however, the expectations of younger workers about their career are different from those held by Baby Boomers when they were at the same stage of their career. Today's younger workers in general do not expect that they will stay for many years in one organisation and have grown up in a period of rapid change. For both reasons, they are impatient to advance. As Mara Swann, EVP of Manpower Group put it "Millennials are used to a faster paced world and ... want varied careers that progress more quickly".

The importance of career development opportunities for retaining key workers

Despite rising unemployment, in most if not all sectors there are still critical skills which are in short supply – lose team members with those skills and businesses can really suffer,

---

[10] Twenge, J.M. (2010). A review of the empirical evidence on generational differences in work attitudes. Journal of Business and Psychology, 25(2), pp.201-210.

and a key reason for employees to leave organisations is a perceived lack of career development opportunities. Retention bonuses and golden handcuffs can work in the short term but given the limited impact of financial incentives, risk becoming a clumsy and expensive tool for addressing such issues.

What can organisations do to encourage career management?

Even without the same degree of influence over the long term career development of their employees they may once have enjoyed, there is still a lot that organisations can do to promote employee career development – well-structured graduate training schemes are still invaluable, whilst laying out career progression pathways, publishing all vacancies internally, actively encouraging internal transfers, promoting opportunities for secondment to a different department or a special project team and allowing time for volunteering are all examples of best practice.

Empowering employees to shape their own role through free time and job crafting

Some organisations have also achieved good results through taking a bottom-up approach. 3M and Google are two well-known examples of companies who have benefited from allowing employees free time to work on their own projects. Whilst many organisations may baulk at going so far, why not encourage employees to think about how they could adapt their own role in a way which could benefit the organisation as well as themselves? Roles can potentially be adapted along different dimensions, e.g. expanding, or changing the people jobholders interact with, removing some tasks and adding others, or (most powerfully) re-thinking the purpose of the role. The approach is sometimes called job crafting[11], invoking the image of the individual creating the right-shape hole to fit the shape of their own "peg".

Job crafting can be a powerful technique for improving job satisfaction and sets team members along the path towards taking responsibility for their own career development. It can also be effective even where the possibilities for internal promotion are limited and allows people to experiment - to see if they enjoy doing something different, before taking a high-risk leap into a wholly new role.

The role of line managers

 The individual is clearly the one with the most at stake in considering their own career, but within organisations, their line manager is often in an unenviable position; frequently looked to by team members for assistance with their career development, whilst simultaneously called upon by the organisation to manage poor performers, stay within

---

[11] Berg, J.M., Dutton, J.E. and Wrzesniewski, A. (2013). Job crafting and meaningful work.

39

budget, hit targets and ensure departmental objectives are achieved.

There are many great managers who develop a strong bond with their employees and armed with tools like those described earlier in this section, find creative ways of helping their employees grow and develop, but their role in employee career management is not an easy one. Employees may recognise that conflicts of interest exist, most obviously where the best individual career move for a top performer is to leave the department or organisation. Tension can also arise when employees become concerned about job security – real dialogue can quickly become replaced by attempts to tell the boss what the employee thinks they want to hear.

In-house career coaches

Some large organisations appoint in-house career coaches, separate from the normal line management chain. These can be very effective in building awareness of the full extent of internal career development opportunities within large organisations, and equipping employees to exploit them, but some of the same difficulties that face line managers may still limit the extent to which they can enable employees to develop true self-awareness and start taking control of their own careers.

Career Management without Boundaries?

 Some organisations go further, employing an approach that in tribute to Michael Arthur's work, I will refer to as **Boundaryless Career Management**. It recognises that modern careers are likely to span multiple organisations and geographical boundaries are becoming less relevant with time. The approach encourages employees to take full responsibility for managing their own careers inside and potentially beyond their current organisation and empowers them by equipping them with the career management skills they will need to do so.

The approach typically involves a combination of training and 1:1 coaching with an external career coach. The aim is to help individuals to develop the key career skills of self-awareness and adaptability, gaining an understanding of:

- their own unique set of career drivers - what is it that can make work most meaningful for them as individuals

- their career aims over the short, medium, and long term

- their career "capital", what it is that they can offer to an employer, identifying any gaps that might hinder them from achieving their goals

- identifying opportunities for achieving their career goals - inside their current organisation, perhaps through voluntary activities and those which may exist outside of their current organisation

- how to effectively market themselves for such internal and external opportunities

A key aspect is confidentiality, using an independent external coach bound by a professional code of ethics. This is important - to discover for yourself, through working with an external coach in a safe, confidential space, that your best next move *may* be outside of the organisation can be exciting and liberating, but to have your line manager suggest this as an idea can provoke anxiety.

Benefits of a Boundaryless Career Management strategy

Employee engagement

Returning to our original observations on the weakened psychological contract, the Boundaryless Career Management approach clarifies and strengthens this considerably; it moves us on from vague promises to something easily understood, communicated and concrete: "*work for us and we will give you all the career management skills and support you need to clarify your goals and achieve them*".

Employees are more motivated and engaged because they understand how the work they are doing contributes to their own career development, have a better grasp on the types of situations in which they flourish, and understanding their strengths better, can play to them. As the proportion of actively engaged and motivated employees increases, performance and employee satisfaction should also improve, with a knock-on effect on customer satisfaction.

Management of change

It is a rational response for employees to be wary of organisational change which may affect their jobs, and fear of change can lead to efforts to undermine or sabotage it. While a boundaryless career management strategy is clearly not a panacea for making change easy, if employees' fear of change can be reduced, it can encourage people to embrace change more willingly.

Attraction, Retention and Employer reputation

Over time, so long as the organisation maintains its commitment to career management, and some "happy leavers" start to spread the word into other organisations – the strategy can boost the organisation's reputation as an enlightened employer, enhancing their ability to attract and retain talent.

Building Trust

In Heather Mills' chapter in this book, she describes the importance and advantages of building trust with employees – this adult to adult approach to empowering employees to take the reins of their own career is an excellent way to do so.

Getting Started: Five Steps to Embracing Boundaryless Career Management

1.	Take Stock	Capture career development opportunities that exist within your organisation, e.g. career progression paths, special projects, action learning, secondments, transfers, CSR Programmes, Volunteer Days etc

2.	Staff Survey	Anonymously survey employees to ask them how the organisation supports career development. What do they think of quantity, quality, extent to which opportunities are publicised, support for internal promotions, transfers, secondments? How much influence do they believe they can have over the nature of their own role?
3.	Train Managers	Train managers on how to have career conversations with their employees. Make sure they are aware of the full scope of opportunities and discuss any barriers. Is the company culture genuinely supportive of employee career development?
4.	Train Employees	Start employees on process of assuming responsibility for their own career development and understanding their personal career goals. Help them build self-awareness about their "career capital" and how they can develop all the skills they will need to achieve their career goals. Encourage them to discuss with their manager how their existing roles can be crafted in line with their career goals and for the good of the organisation.
5.	Push the Boundaries	Should career development be confined within your organisation's own walls or should you take the logical leap to thinking about careers that span organisations? Once the limits of internal career development have been reached, what is better - happy leavers and an enhanced employer reputation or disengaged stayers? A halfway house may be to extend career management to embrace sister or partner organisations.

Summary

This chapter has explored the realities of today's employment landscape and what really motivates employees. Equipping team members with the skills they need to achieve fulfilment in their career can create a win / win situation – with happier employees and a high-performance organisation. Organisations can do a lot to facilitate this, but there are limits on what managers can do on their own - the real responsibility for career management lies with the individual.

An approach which recognises this and supports employees to manage their careers within and beyond their current employer can be particularly effective in a rapidly changing landscape. It also reintroduces clarity and relevance into the psychological contract – a good way to re-engage with employees and build trust.

> ### The New Psychological Contract
>
> *"Work for us and we will give you all the career management skills and support you need to clarify your goals and achieve them"*

About the Author

Michelle Bailey BA (Hons) MCIPD

www.peopleessentials.co.uk

Michelle has more than 25 years' experience as an HR professional. She uses her knowledge, experience and sense of humour to help organisations engage employees and customers alike.

She started her HR career in large corporates before developing a passion for working with SME's and setting up People Essentials, which has been running successfully for more than 10 years.

A fan of employee feedback Michelle has developed an employee survey platform which clients use to improve decision making and increase productivity.

Michelle is an active member of the CIPD chairing the Special Interest Group for independent consultants and in 2020 took on the role of chair for the Thames Valley Branch.

How to cure your productivity problem

By Michelle Bailey

In my experience most organisations are looking for a shortcut to better productivity.

> "Productivity isn't everything,
> but in the long run it is almost
> everything.
>
> Krugman 1994

UK productivity has been a problem for years. In 2016, UK productivity was significantly lower than every G7 country (except Japan) – put another way UK employees have to work until Friday while French and German workers can produce the same amount and finish work on Thursday.

"with statistics still showing that on average only 30% of the workforce is engaged it's clear we still have work to do"

Better productivity is about maximising output, with the least effort, it's about working smarter not working harder. Getting the best from your people is therefore of critical importance.

In our ongoing quest to work out how to get people to perform their best most of us have realised we can't make or just expect people to give their all. We've also learned that productivity is an even bigger challenge during times of change when uncertainty disrupts the status quo and creates a natural resistance to change.

Figure 1 Exploring the relationship between engagement and productivity

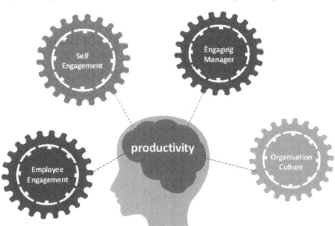

Studies[12] have found that when organisations increase employee engagement it's not just productivity that improves. However, with statistics still showing that on average only 30% of the workforce is engaged it's clear we still have work to do.

That's why I was intrigued by an article suggesting it was more important for organisations to have self-engaged employees than engaging managers and why, in this chapter, I decided to explore this conundrum.

This chapter considers how individuals, managers and organisation culture impact employee engagement and how better engagement can help you manage change and improve productivity (figure 1).

what does engagement look like?

One thing I've noticed about people who are engaged is that their energy spreads, people are drawn to them, their energy and enthusiasm infects and stimulates others.

> "You sort of smell it, don't you, that engagement of people as people."
>
> Lord David Currie

There's one definition of employee engagement I have always loved and it's that you can 'smell' it. It may sound daft at first, but you really

---

[12] Engage for Success: The Evidence. Employee Engagement Taskforce "Nailing the evidence" workgroup November 2012

can! There's lots of evidence showing that emotions have a scent which influences us without our realising it[13].

I've smelt it in many organisations I have worked with – there's always a buzz when you walk in, you can sense the energy, there's a hum of conversation, you can hear and see people talking about work stuff in a way that shows it matters to them. People look like they enjoy being there.

why do people have different levels of engagement?

Even when they have the same manager and the same job people can have different levels of engagement – and that difference can be attributed to their personality.

Personality is a product of a number of things; Of genetics (nature), environment (nurture) and your life experience. All combine and evolve over time to determine how you think, feel, and behave.

Some personalities have traits that help them engage more easily than others. These are likely to include personality traits (figure 2) such as optimism, positivity, resilience, confidence – incidentally a lot of the behaviours we associate with people who are engaged.

Even then engagement is not a constant. Can you say that you feel engaged all of the time - I challenge you to think of anyone you know who can?

---

[13] The sense of Smell in Humans is More Powerful Than We Think, Marta Zaraska, Discover Magazine. October 2017

positive

optimistic

energetic

confident

reliable

assertive

hardworking

resilient

Figure 2 Behaviours of an engaged employee

Events at work can affect everyone's engagement and productivity levels.

I've seen the productivity of the best performers wobble when they feel overwhelmed by too much to do, impending deadlines, difficult customers, boring tasks, a disagreement with a colleague or the loss of a contract.

Then of course what's going on outside work impacts productivity as much as what's happening in the workplace.

We have seen some interesting differences in engagement levels from the employee surveys we have carried out with organisations too:

- Team leaders, managers and senior managers are more engaged than their employees.
- New starters are more engaged than longer serving colleagues
- Engagement levels tend to decline with length of service
- Older employees tend to be more engaged than younger colleagues

51

These findings are backed up by other studies[14] which also found engagement levels varied according to gender, ethnicity and disability.

Disengagement however results from more than just a bad day, we can all have that, it results from having one bad day after another.

is self-engagement important?

It's hard to engage without making some effort yourself because, in the end, no-one can make you engage, or become more engaged, that's your choice.

The decision to engage is personal – as an individual you decide what's most important, how much of yourself you want to give and where you want to invest yourself. Engagement varies between individuals according to their values, skills, personality and aspirations and varies with personal and work circumstances.

If you have a 'bad day' at work the sense of obligation and commitment that come from being engaged is generally unchanged. When your bad day becomes the norm trust erodes and engagement falls. People who are able to self-engage may prove to be more resilient in these circumstances but engagement and productivity will fail longer term.

A self-engaged employee doesn't always make a loyal employee either. They may be committed to performing well, but are likely only to have made a rational commitment to your organisation. I've worked with several organisations

[14] Employee Engagement A review of current thinking: Institute for Employment Studies 2009

struggling with high employee turnover because their culture didn't encourage loyalty. Focused on their personal goals their high performers looked for 'better' opportunities as soon as they felt the organisation couldn't meet their needs.

"A self-engaged employee doesn't always make a loyal employee"

If employers rely wholly on their employees to self-engage there is no reciprocal relationship or basis to encourage employee loyalty.

Some people may be better equipped to self-engage than others but that doesn't mean they will be the best or most productive performers. Neither does it mean that other people can't or won't engage. A diverse workforce with a range of backgrounds, personality traits and experience, appropriately supported, is more likely to achieve the highest levels of engagement and productivity.

Research by McKinsey[15] found companies in the top quartile of gender diversity were 15 percent more likely to have financial returns above the industry average and those in the top quartile of racial/ethnic diversity were 35 percent more likely to have financial returns above the industry average.

True engagement is based on a reciprocal relationship in which parties make a rational and emotional commitment to each other. Good employers recognise and accept there will

[15] Diversity Matters. McKinsey & Company. February 2015.

be times when employee's productivity fluctuates but a prolonged drop in performance is a sign of disengagement. Our experience is that this is a more likely to be a regular occurrence where there is no commitment to you as an employer.

how do managers impact engagement?

When I look back on my career my roles all shared some common features. The organisations I worked for as an employee were all going through some kind of change including massive restructures, takeovers and ambitious growth strategies.

I started each job enthused, excited and engaged. But I knew then and I know now that what made the difference in the longer term was my manager.

I see this reflected in the majority of the employee surveys I run for my clients. Employees with the highest levels of engagement consistently report positive scores for statements including 'I trust my manager' and 'my manager cares about me'. Where people reported low levels of engagement, they had consistently lower scores for managers in respect of trust and fairness.

On their own managers aren't a driver of engagement – their value comes in creating conditions that encourage and enable people to engage. Having a good manager doesn't automatically mean employees will be engaged but will reduce the chance that they will be disengaged.

Considering the statistics that only 30% of employees are engaged it's probably fair to suggest that managers are not currently doing a great job supporting people to engage.

managers need to be engaged

Managers are people too and you can't expect them to engage your employees if they are not engaged themselves. This means creating a workplace that empowers and enables them to engage.

There are many models for successful engagement one of which is the 4 enablers of engagement identified by Engage for Success[16] (Figure 3).

This model suggests employees, including managers, should be provided with a clearly defined purpose and objectives so they can relate the work they do to the bigger picture. They need feedback, coaching and the opportunity to learn and grow. Good communication and trusted relationships will give people the opportunity to affect decisions that affect them and the work they do.

Figure 3 Engage for Success 4 enablers for Employee Engagement

ENGAGE FOR SUCCESS
4 Enablers for Employee Engagement

| STRATEGIC NARRATIVE | ENGAGING MANAGERS | EMPLOYEE VOICE | INTEGRITY |

[16] Engaging for success (the MacLeod report) BIS 2009

55

This makes people feel psychologically safe and is as important as providing them with interesting and challenging work to do.

How engaged your managers are is just one key to engaging your employees the other is whether they have the skills to do so.

managers need to be capable

Gallup research[17] found that one in 10 people are naturally great managers and that with the right coaching and development another 2 in 10 have the talent to be successful. With managers in most companies leading an average 8 employees that should mean there is enough talent to go round.

Engagement is about connecting with people, about understanding them as individuals their likes, dislikes and motivations etc. The most effective managers we have seen treat each person in their team differently according to what they know about them - inside and outside of work. They use this knowledge when they give feedback and recognition, to create opportunities for learning and tailor the support they give them.

Managers with these soft skills can create the right conditions for people to self-engage and enable people who don't find it so easy to self-engage too. In my experience people can't sustain engagement without the support of their manager –

---

[17] State of The American Manager Gallup Inc 2015

not without some negative impact on performance, health or wellbeing.

We have seen that when people trust their managers, they are more engaged and in times of change feel safe to experiment, take (calculated) risks, share their feelings and support each other.

how does culture impact engagement?

In our experience, and according to our employee survey database, the majority of people join organisations and start new jobs engaged. The trouble is, as our surveys also show, it's not so easy to keep them engaged.

Lack of trust, unfairness, poor management and job insecurity are known to damage engagement – especially during times of change. People find change stressful mostly because the uncertainty and lack of control makes them feel insecure, they doubt themselves, lose confidence and feel vulnerable. The fall back has always been to make people feel safe by removing ambiguity, uncertainty and risk. This is not realistic in today's environment when change and instability is a constant. We need to find a different way.

Creating an organisation culture of safe uncertainty is one approach.

The concept of safe uncertainty comes from work by Barry Mason in the field of Family Therapy. He found that by shifting peoples' focus, from just finding a solution to (fix) a problem, they were enabled to be more experimental, innovative and resilient in dealing with change.

The following explains how Masons model can be applied to workplace culture (figure 4).

Adapted from Mason 1993 Safe Uncertainty Framework

Figure 4 Safe Uncertainty framework

In a culture of **Safe Uncertainty** people understand they cannot know everything and they need to keep learning and improving if they want to succeed. Information about the purpose and direction of the organisation is clear and shared with people so they know what they need to do and why, even if they don't always know how. Managers are open and responsive to feedback and people are trusted to do their jobs. Employees are encouraged to ask questions, be open, try new things, take risks and talk openly to each other including sharing concerns and fears. They take on board each other's views, ideas and opinions and adapt theirs accordingly.

Safety and certainty are two very different things. As the covid-19 pandemic has demonstrated life is uncertain – as employers and individuals we have very little, if any, control over it. When we feel safe we are more able to embrace uncertainty, engagement and maintain and grow employee productivity

What's most important for productivity self-engaging employees or great managers?

The answer is neither – it's not an either or situation.

Engagement benefits both employees and employers and achieving it must also be a shared responsibility. Employees can only sustain productivity and engagement when they take an active role and managers actively support them to make it happen.

Some people are good at engagement, but most aren't. Most people cannot stay engaged on their own. Some managers are good at engagement but most need support to maintain their own engagement and to develop the skills to help others engage.

A strong organisation culture will align peoples actions and behaviours as it is clear what is expected and what they are working toward. Just remember that a strong culture does not automatically mean it's the best culture and therefore strengths and weaknesses, healthy and unhealthy practices will also be reinforced.

A weak culture will lead to a misalignment of behaviours, without clarity people will do what they want to do or what they feel is the right thing to do. In any case if there is not some fit between individual behaviour, manager and organisation culture then engagement and productivity will not be sustained.

Is there a short cut to productivity?

The simple answer is no.

However, if you help your employees improve their level of engagement, even by just a small amount, you will see a significant change in individual and organisation productivity.

A culture of safe uncertainty creates a pathway to productivity and change. Change, learning and innovation is risky. If people don't feel safe to take the risk they won't try, they will disengage. When you focus on creating an environment that encourages and supports people to engage, you will create the conditions for 'good work' and also make them feel safe.

Your employee's role is to understand their strengths, share information about their interests and aspirations and identify where they need help to engage.

Managers need to support this inclusive culture and behave in a fair and trustworthy way. They need to be clear about what the business is trying to achieve, how each individual contributes and understand their employees well enough to be able to support them to engage.

We encourage employers to apply Masons model in employee surveys and use direct questions about psychological safety to help them identify how strong their culture is and where they can make improvements.

Where do I start?

Managers and organisations achieve the best productivity when they create a culture and working conditions that make people feel safe.

Take some time to reflect, observe and ask for feedback from your people to help you understand how safe they feel and where you can make improvements.

You may find the following questions helpful in doing this:

1. Where does your organisation culture sit in Masons framework?
2. How well do you know your people? The more you know about them the more effective you will be in helping them engage.
   a. How (psychologically) safe do people feel?
   b. What would you need to do differently to encourage your employees to speak up and voice their opinions and ideas?
   c. What changes would encourage people to be more open about mistakes and when things go wrong.
   d. What could you do to encourage your employees to take more (calculated) risks at work?
3. How can you encourage people to take (more) responsibility for their own engagement?
4. What (additional) skills do you (managers) need to develop to support employees to engage?

Few organisations will fit neatly in to one of Masons four quadrants, there is likely to be some overlap with one or more. You may also find that different parts of your organisation operate in different quadrants.

Don't just focus on the negatives - make time to explore the strengths of your organisation too. Consider what you can learn from them, how can you use them to support weaker areas and how to maintain and improve them.

And finally remember you don't need to come up with all the answers, indeed you shouldn't. Now is the perfect time to engage your people in the process. Involve them in identifying where to focus and the best actions to get the results you want.

About the Author

Heather Mills MA HRM MCIPD

www.ducksouphr.co.uk

Heather Mills spent the earlier part of her career in Oxford in the public and not for profit sectors before moving into the private sector.

25 years' experience of working with different organisational cultures and management styles has shown her that the only way to achieve a lasting benefit to the bottom line is by treating staff with respect, communicating openly, being transparent, encouraging learning and enabling staff.

She is now on a mission to spread the word and teach SMEs through professional HR support how to develop a winning culture and how to lead and manage their staff to be more productive, more innovative, more flexible and more committed to increasing profits for the business.

Through her business, Duck Soup HR, Heather now works with regular and new clients in the private and public sectors.

How do you maintain workplace trust in a changing world?

By Heather Mills

> *'In times of great uncertainty, leaders are faced with one of two choices. Freeze to the point of inaction, allowing uncertainty to damage culture, performance, results, and significantly slow a return to greatness. Or, transform fear into engagement, execute with excellence, use the uncertainty as a time to actually increase trust, and help everyone in the organization prepare to do more with less.'*
>
> Stephen M R Covey

Introduction

I know, from 25 years in HR, that the companies that do well are the ones who have created a culture of trust. Yet in my experience, in the face of uncertainty, most organisations fall somewhere between inaction and transforming the fear into engagement.

What if I told you that if you build trust with your employees, they'll say good things about you. And when they do, consumers will believe them. And when people trust a company, they buy their products, they pay a higher price over comparable products, and they recommend them to their friends.

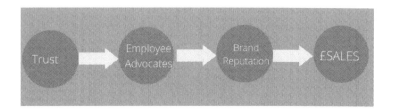

But we know all this, don't we? We've been talking about trust for so long that the work of the late great Stephen Covey (businessman, educator and author, renowned for his work on trust) is now being taken forward by his son, Stephen M R Covey (above).

Trust is an increasingly important issue in the world of work. As the world becomes more remote and technology-led, so the ability to trust others becomes increasingly important. Let me ask you something. I'd like you to examine your own level of trust at the moment. How much trust do you have right now in, say, the government, or large corporations, or the media? How much trust do you have in your senior managers and your staff? Do you think you are alone in how you feel?

The bad news for us is that, after measuring Trust for the last 20 years, Edelman[18] says that in 2020 trust is at an all-time low.

But it isn't all doom and gloom. Edelman has found that the greatest opportunity to improve levels of trust is with organisations. People are looking to organisations to improve this situation, not because they trust them, but because they see business as the only institution competent to do so. And people don't often trust institutions or organisations – they trust the people in those organisations. If we consider the elements of the Trust Equation – credibility, reliability, intimacy and self-orientation - (more on this later), we can see that Companies are often described as credible and reliable, but Intimacy and Self-Orientation are specific to individuals.

Sally Stiegler (read her chapter on Culture) a Senior HR Professional who has worked with many big brands including Mars and Coca-Cola says, 'From my experience big brands work hard on consumer trust in brand, but take employee trust for granted, with little focus or understanding on what builds or destroys trust'.

So what happened to trust? Did business leaders forget all that they knew about the importance of trust, or maybe they never learnt it in the first place? And does it matter?

---

[18] The Edelman Trust Barometer is an exploration of trust in business, not for profits, government and media, surveying 34,000 people in 28 different countries

How would you define trust?

It's difficult to define trust because trust is an emotion and it is in constant negotiation. It has to be earned. It is socially constructed, it depends on an individual's history, culture, experience, and so on.

If you have trust, it means that you are willing to take a risk, to make yourself vulnerable to a person or organisation because you believe that they have good intentions towards you. You can think of trust as confidence, distrust as suspicion.

'Trust is the glue of life. It's the most essential ingredient in effective communication. It's the foundational principle that holds all relationships.' Stephen Covey

For staff at work, trust can manifest itself in feelings for employers such as knowing that leaders are on "their side," they will be treated fairly and with respect and setbacks will be viewed favourably or at least not with particularly negative consequences.

A good explanation of the feeling of trust is the Trust Equation developed by David Maister 'The Trusted Advisor' 2000.

The Trust Equation

$$\text{Trustworthiness} = \frac{\text{Credibility} + \text{Reliability} + \text{Intimacy}}{\text{Self Orientation}}$$

The Trust Equation can be explained as follows[19]: three numerators are credibility, reliability and intimacy. The aim is to increase these to increase trust. The denominator is self-orientation, which we aim to reduce to increase trust.

Credibility

Credibility is about words, simply 'do they know what they are talking about?'

In order to practice in HR, I have had to pass exams and get tested to gain the required qualifications.

Reliability

Reliability is about action, doing what we say we will do.

A former colleague, Dan, was consistently late to meetings where a time had been clearly agreed. It eroded trust. When Dan would say he'd meet me at a time and a place there was a part of me that knew it was unlikely to happen – I

---

[19] Roderick Yapp 22 October 2015 'The Trust Equation'

experienced a reduced level of trust in Dan. If he couldn't get to a meeting on time, what else was he going to fail to do?

Intimacy

Intimacy is about emotions – creating environments where people feel comfortable to speak up.

I remember an occasion where I told a senior manager that a member of staff had expressed a concern about part of their job. My intention was to resolve the issue for the member of staff. The senior manager reacted by asking 'Who said that?'. I told them, albeit reluctantly, and the member of staff was hauled over the coals. I quickly learnt not to trust that senior manager and I suspect the poor member of staff also lost trust in me.

Self-Orientation

Self-Orientation is the only denominator in the equation. It is about focus – there is no "I" in team. If people sense that you don't care about them or their needs, they will not trust you.

This goes for organisations as well. Does my organisation train me and help me to improve so that I can advance my career? Or does it just expect me to deliver for which I get a salary in return?

These factors are worth considering from a personal point of view as well as from the perspective of your organisation. It is usually people within organisations, not the organisations themselves, that people trust.

People have to demonstrate intimacy and self-orientation. It is why doctors have a simple criteria for making decisions – 'put the patient's welfare first'. This builds trust in their profession and their institutions. It is vital to the long-term success of the organisation and is part of a virtuous circle. Many companies say that they 'put the customer first' but if they don't back it up with their actions - it undermines trust in their organisation.

Trust in business requires good scores across the board. Leadership requires us to live these values by example. If we do, they percolate through the organisation resulting in a 'trusted company or brand'. This builds long-term success.

Does Workplace Trust matter?

To me, trust means working with a team of people who understand the goals of their company and their roles. Everyone works hard to fill those roles effectively because they know that if everyone is aligned, everyone succeeds. This includes not only knowing your role, but also how it connects to the roles of others. Trust in the workplace boils down internalizing the idea that a company is a team of interconnected people that have to move together to be most effective, rather than islands of individuals jockeying for position.'

Marco Rogers, Senior Software Engineer, Yammer

How many of us have worked in organisations where people are selective with the information they share, only using it to promote themselves or their cause, perhaps with a little bit of spin. Where people work in silos instead of talking to each other, and work is duplicated or departments actually work against each other. Where everyone is trying to keep hold of their positions, watching their backs and hiding mistakes in case they look bad. Or trying to get the credit for themselves rather than furthering the organisation's success.

How many of us have known the frustration of having genuinely good ideas blocked? Or tried to navigate complicated politics, reluctant to call out unsafe working practices, breaches of ethics or illegal behaviour, for fear of being seen as a trouble maker? Or been bogged down with endless processes, reviews and sanctions used by untrusting managers.

I can remember attending a monthly meeting of everyone who worked in a building together. It had a loose aim of improving communication. It was a group of about 15 people, some very junior, who all worked in different teams, chaired by the most senior manager who also worked in the building, and attended by the other senior managers. You could have cut the atmosphere with a knife. The format involved going round the room like the 'creeping death' and everyone had to report on their team. The reluctance to contribute was palpable. No'one knew what they were supposed to say, and if they said the wrong thing, they were shouted down.

It's exhausting. This is what happens when trust is low. And the result is, unsurprisingly, apathy and reduced productivity. Energy and attention is diverted away from the strategic purpose of the organisation. Employees are more likely to be looking to change job and are much less likely to be an advocate for their employer.

Imagine if all that energy was redirected towards productivity and innovation for the company. This is what happens when trust is high. When people are trusted to get on with the job, they tend to engage more with the company and align with its mission. When trust exists in a team, everyone works together to excel to maintain that trust. And when trust exists in an organisation, managers don't need to spend their time on bureaucracy and can instead clear a path for their team, and inspire their staff to truly collaborate, solve problems and increase speed and productivity. Overhead reduces and the trust enables the transfer of tacit knowledge, in an age where we are told that the flow of information is the competitive advantage.[20]

The Edelman Trust Barometer has consistently found that the way businesses treat their employees is one of the most important factors influencing public trust. A loss of trust by employees can have much wider effects on the reputation, revenues and perceived legitimacy of an organisation.

The Hilton Hotel has achieved this holy grail over the last decade through its staff, with a simple philosophy to 'treat team members of every position as well as the guests that stay in the hotel'. The company sets itself apart from other employers by being a great host to its own people in three key ways: by creating Purpose From the Top; designing For All Programmes; and developing For All People Leaders.

---

[20] Stephen M R Covey 'The Speed of Trust

Great Place to Work[21] research shows turnover, productivity, brand ambassadorship and customer service are all positively impacted by creating a great workplace For All. And it pays off in significantly stronger annual revenue growth. Hilton's own analysis shows a relationship between team member experience and business metrics, including customer satisfaction, property loyalty, and overall guest service.

Other signs confirm that being better for all their people has been better for Hilton's business. In recent years, JD Power has rated Hilton among the top five hotels in North America on its Guest Satisfaction Index. Company profits are up more than 20% year-over- year. And shareholders are seeing the benefits, with earnings per share more than doubling over the same period last year.

How to Create Trust in the Workplace?

OK, so we know that trust is at an all-time low, we know that the world is looking to business to re-establish trust, and we have established that it is not businesses that people trust, but the people within them. We have discovered that high trust organisations are faster and more productive than those with low trust. And that if business leaders and managers trust the staff, they recommend the business and customers buy from the business at a premium as a direct result.

So how do business leaders create trust in the workplace? Let's consider the steps that we can take to build trust.

---

[21] Fortune 100 Best Places to Work 2020

Step 1 Acknowledge that trust is an issue

Make a conscious decision as a leadership team that trust is important and that the organisation can and wants to do better.

Take time to reflect, observe and ask for feedback from your staff to help you identify where and how to improve trust. Michelle Bailey's chapter 'Solving the Productivity Problem' contains some useful questions to ask about psychological safety.

Step 2 Work on Self

Businesses can really benefit from using the Trust Equation to help identify issues and opportunities to focus on to increase trust. Leaders, assess your own Trust Quotient and that of your managers. Look at the results. What are the trends? Are there any common issues to investigate further? What opportunities do you have to increase trust?

Leaders and managers, learn about the benefits of an environment of Trust, look at the Trust Equation and how to gain trust and role model the desired behaviours of credibility, reliability, intimacy and the correct self-orientation. Help them meet any gaps and develop these skills through individual and group coaching.

You can assess your own Trust Quotient on the Trusted Advisor website, but why not have a go here and score yourself out of 10 in each of the 4 areas.

Covey[20] believes that these 13 behaviours go a long way towards building an environment of trust : talk straight, demonstrate respect, create transparency, right wrongs, show loyalty, deliver results, get better, confront reality, clarify expectations, practice accountability, listen first, keep commitments and extend trust.

How well do you use the 13 behaviours identified by Covey?

Step 3 Organisational Systems

Most high profile losses of trust have originated with shortcomings in organisational culture and the link between behaviour and values – where responsibility ultimately lies with senior leadership.

First, does the organisation have a set of values and behaviours that they will adhere to? If not, it is difficult for staff to see that they are acting with integrity, consistency and predictability. Are they in tune with employees' values? The most effective values are ones which are simple and easy to translate into day-to-day practice and are backed up through performance appraisals and other corporate procedures.

Fair treatment is important for trust. There is an expectation that organisation-wide processes, such as pay setting, promotion decisions or appraisal, operate efficiently and fairly.

Do staff feel that the organisation has their interests at heart. Do they train them and give them opportunities to learn skills and progress?

What does the organisation do to benefit society?

Amend organisational processes to attract, nurture and reward trust. For example:

- Define organisational values based around the concept of trust and keep these at the forefront of business decisions and messaging
- Devise KPIs around demonstrating credibility, reliability, intimacy and benevolence so that your people work towards that and reward people appropriately
- Advertise the organisational values of trust when recruiting staff
- Look at your organisation's policies. Do they encourage trust?
- Challenge leaders and managers who do not display the right behaviours

Step 4 Communication and Involvement

Communications and involvement in decision-making are important ingredients in building employee trust. Survey staff. How strong is the employee voice? How meaningful is consultation? Do staff feel safe to challenge? Is it ok to admit that you've made a mistake? Can people be honest about progress towards deadlines and evaluating when things haven't gone well in order to learn and improve?

Step 5 Rinse and Repeat

Trust is crucial to the bottom line. Business leaders need to make trust part of the company culture and its DNA. It must be an ongoing process to be most productive, one that is constantly reviewed and revisited in order to develop and maintain trust from staff and trust from customers and the wider society.

Conclusion

In today's economy, an organization's brand and customer loyalty rest in the hands of its employees more than ever.

If you're like most organizations, you will have spent a lot of time, effort and money trying to improve your brand, without reaping the rewards. You may have focussed on repositioning your corporate identity, renaming your products and trying to recapture your customer's imaginations.

But, for leaders who want to maximise engagement, innovation, productivity and brand perception, then look at Hilton as an example and start with your staff. Improving and maintaining workplace trust is paramount.

Developing trust is possible if leaders and managers are not afraid to look at themselves and be honest about the reality.

High trust businesses are more resilient and react more quickly in our constantly changing world. The future looks challenging, but trust can be maintained if kept on the agenda and with frank discussion between leaders and the workforce about how to navigate it.

About the Author

Shirley has been passionate about the changing world of work since studying the impact of technology on organisations and individuals at Digital Equipment, a leading IT company in the 1980s. She has been involved in research with the Future Work Forum at Henley Management College, and was Development Director of the Telework Association. She has created and delivered management and employee training for many organisations, including distance learning for the Chartered Institute of Personnel and Development. She wrote the Lawpack 'Working from Home' kit.

Shirley is a Chartered member of the CIPD and has a psychology degree and an MBA from the Open University. She is currently developing the website http://www.betterwaystowork.co.uk to capture the history, growth and future of new ways of working, including Working From Home.

Working From Home for business survival – but which survive?

By Shirley Borrett

Working from home (WFH) has been steadily increasing over the last three decades. In 2003 a fifth of UK employees working full time and a quarter of those working part time had some type of flexible working, including home working[22]. By 2019 figures just for home working had increased to one third of employees in some sectors (Figure 1)[23]

Then the coronavirus pandemic arrived. Traditional advice to run pilots, conduct change management programmes, and train managers, became irrelevant. Within a week of the UK Government exhorting everyone to "work from home if you can", hundreds of thousands of people changed their working practice. Before Corona many people commuted to an office to sit at a desk and send emails to their colleagues a few

---

22 (Office for National Statistics, 2004b)
23
https://www.ons.gov.uk/employmentandlabourmarket/peopleinwork/employmentandemployeetypes/articles/technologyintensityandhomeworkingintheuk/2020-05-01

meters or a couple of floors away. During coronavirus lockdown they sit at kitchen tables, or in spare rooms, garden sheds or corner of a bedroom, sending the same emails to colleagues also sitting in their own homes.

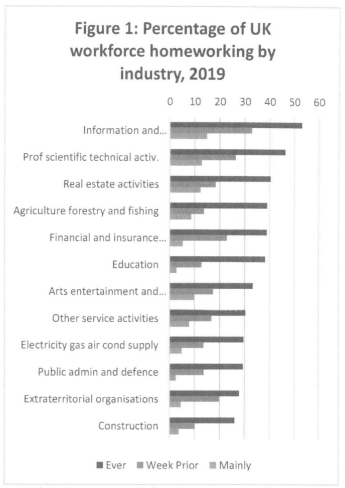

Figure 1: Percentage of UK workforce homeworking by industry, 2019

Coronavirus is not an entirely unique event as far as WFH is concerned. Home working has been a way to enable businesses to survive in previous challenging times. In March 1990 Digital, a technology company then in the forefront of innovative ways of working, had a major fire at their Basingstoke office, at The Crescent[24]

Despite extensive damage which would take months to repair, within 24 hours the 'office' was operational again. Some people worked from other offices, but many were able to work from home. Other examples include transport strikes, heavy snow, ash clouds and, perhaps most significantly, the 2001 terrorist attack of 9/11. These situations all saw employees retreat to their homes to work as best they could. Many self-employed people work this way all the time. But coronavirus lockdown is unique in providing a giant widespread experiment in home working, across many industrial sectors and a huge range of job roles.

How successful WFH is in such diverse situations depends on many things, including the individual circumstances of each employee. Some homes have what were previously considered essential conditions, for successful home working:

- a spare room, study, or garden office, with a door to provide both quiet working conditions and a separation of work from home life.

Many modern homes are unsuitable, having a limited number of small rooms. Younger employees living with parents or in shared accommodation, find working from home particularly difficult. The pandemic entreaty to "work from home" also applied to children, as schools shut for all but a few. So there goes another piece of longstanding WFH advice: it is not a

---

[24] (https://www.youtube.com/watch?v=YXR8cUhgA14)

substitute for childcare. The homeworker should have care arrangements in place so that they can concentrate on work. Not possible for many in coronavirus lockdown, hence the appearance of inquisitive toddlers in business Zoom meetings and live TV interviews!

After five months, it seems to be working adequately for many. Some businesses would have collapsed if their people were unable to continue at least some work activity. Without meeting face to face, without their usual structures, and with less hands-on supervision, many employees and managers have just got on with it.

To the surprise of many, home working, even in such extraordinary circumstances, has been successful. Does this mean the case for WFH as a business tool is proven, not just for an unprecedented pandemic, but also as a new way of working? It seems too early to reach a definite conclusion.

WFH success, as well as depending on individual employee circumstances, is also linked to management competence. Before Corona, managers of flexible workers were exhorted to trust employees, and to treat people as grown-ups so that they would respond in responsible, adult ways. Many managers, whilst paying lip-service to the idea of trusting people, were uncomfortable, with just letting

Working From Home success is linked to management competence.

people get on with the work. Their automatic response to requests for home working, or even just flexible working, was NO. They believed in the principle of McGregor's Theory X, that people are inherently lazy and, left to their own devices without incentives or close supervision, will do as little as they can get away with. No doubt in this giant experiment, some of them will have been proved correct. But many have been surprised to be proved wrong.

Conversely, McGregor's Theory Y postulates that people generally are self-motivated, loyal, and want to do a good job. Coronavirus has given those people the opportunity to show that they can be as productive, if not more so, managing their own time, organising their own work, and collaborating in their own way. Managers meanwhile have faced a steep learning curve in managing people remotely. *'Managing Tomorrow's Worker'* research sponsored by Microsoft[25] in 2005, unexpectedly found that managers of remote workers do not require additional skills to managers of co-located staff. Remote working, including home working, requires more management time and can be a challenge, but the skills are the same. Managers of people working from home do need good traditional, well-recognised management skills:

- Communication
- Leadership
- Planning
- Resource allocation
- Performance management
- Objective setting
- Motivating
- Coaching
- Team building

---

[25] Research by Future Work Forum at Henley Management College

Top of the list for managers with people working from home is communication. Two-way, open, honest, regular communication, is one of the key components of successful home working programmes. Good managers will do this already with all their staff. Hence good managers generally have fewer problems coping with remote workers than those who rely on command and control methods.

Cultural change is needed in many organisations to encourage trust and open communication. Concentrating on what people achieve, rather than how long they work is often impossible to predict or monitor, especially when home schooling is a disrupting factor. Reward schemes should reflect the emphasis on outcomes, not input. This must be good management practice, and good business, whether people are office based or home based. Rewarding achievement, rather than hours worked, makes sense for all parties. However, achievement can be difficult to measure in many jobs, so measuring hours worked has been

"Achievement can be difficult to measure in many jobs, so measuring hours worked has been the easy solution."

the easy solution. Less than 20% of the managers in the Henley/Microsoft study had any training related to managing flexible workers –there is little evidence that this has changed since 2005.

In the 2020 pandemic it seems that as a strategy for business continuity and even survival, WFH works. At least to some extent. At least for a few months. At least for some organisations and some people. Whether that will prove to be the case longer term is currently unknowable. However, apart from the course of Covid-19 itself, the following factors will influence whether WFH is good for business.

Productivity

There are studies showing that productivity increases when working from home. Research conducted before the pandemic by the Harvard Business Review found that workers at the US Patent and Trade Office improved their productivity by 4.4 per cent. Other reports suggest productivity suffers.

But business success relies on more than just productivity. IBM was an early adopter of working from home:

> In 2009, a report boasted that '40 per cent of IBM's 386,000 employees in 173 countries have no office at all'. (The company also saved $2 billion on office space.) But, in March 2017, IBM started to reverse the policy. Commentators mentioned that productivity might have improved, but not 'collaborative efficiency', for example, the speed at which a group solves a problem.

At this stage it is impossible to generalise but, whilst confusing, this picture at least indicates that for many organisations, productivity increases are achievable. WFH does not automatically result in poorer business outcomes. Organisations need to identify the outcomes that are aiming for so that they have a clear target.

Employee engagement

There is little data on the degree to which home working employees are engaged with their organisation, or loyal to its management. This will no doubt emerge over time. But there are studies indicating that some employees want to continue homeworking, at least some of the time, once lockdown and coronavirus anxiety diminishes.

According to a survey for the Business Clean Air Taskforce (includes Philips, Uber and Canary Wharf group), almost nine out of ten Britons who have worked from home in lockdown would like to continue in some way. Many organisations also indicate that they will continue with WFH. A Gartner Survey in July 2020[26] reveals 82% of company leaders plan to allow employees to work remotely in the future.

Figure 2: Company leader intentions regarding flexible working after COVID-19

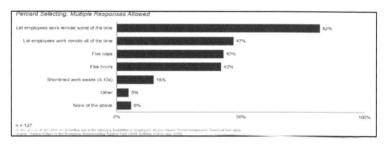

This likely feeds into loyalty and longer job tenure, resulting in savings from lower staff turnover – those wanting to continue WFH are unlikely to leave an organisation that supports it for one that does not.

Stress and work life balance

HR News, quoting from 4Com research suggests that:

---

[26] https://www.gartner.com/en/newsroom/press-releases/2020-07-14-gartner-survey-reveals-82-percent-of-company-leaders-plan-to-allow-employees-to-work-remotely-some-of-the-time

"… nearly six in ten Brits (59%) believe working from home has improved their working lives, whereas less than half this amount (23%) claimed working from home hasn't had any impact on their working life and just 18% said working from home had, in fact, made their work life worse."

This data seems encouraging, since home working at this time often includes the additional stress of coping with isolation, or home schooling, or cramped/shared working spaces, plus anxiety about Covid-19 itself. If employees see the opportunity of WFH as having a positive effect on their lives, despite these additional problems, they may see WFT in 'normal' circumstances as life enhancing.

It is worth considering that during the pandemic, reference to working FROM home actually refers to working AT home. Earlier statistics and reports referring to WFH usually meant that the home was the base from which the employee managed their role. They were working at home some of the time, but also sometimes working at a central location or perhaps at a client's premises, as well as working in public spaces like cafes, hotel lobbies, libraries or at local collaboration spaces.

The pandemic experience of WFH is more restricted, probably more stressful, and mental health considerations critical. Hence managers need to be practising good communication, good listening, and checking regularly on how their people are coping.

Cost implications

If more employees work from home then organisations may be able to reduce their dependence and expenditure on expensive central offices. The extent to which these savings are offset by costs associated with creating more dispersed meeting hubs, or upgrading technology for remote access may affect cost decisions. Although the death of large central HQ buildings is no doubt greatly exaggerated, business survival may depend on organisations taking a more critical look at the way offices are used and how they could be better designed and managed to cater for those uses.

Caveats

Politicians and governments introduce policies and make decisions, we hope, so that the economy, and the population, thrive and prosper. More widespread adoption of WFH by a significant proportion of companies and organisations in the UK could have considerable, and probably unintended, consequences.

- The value of city centre office buildings and large-scale central shopping complexes could drop significantly as organisations disperse and individuals shop online or locally. Houses in towns and cities might be less in demand, whilst those in rural areas become more desirable, and more expensive. People can live further from the central base of their organisation if they don't need to travel there regularly. Even in August 2020, whilst many aspects of lockdown are still in place, estate agents report

125% increase in enquiries for homes in the countryside.

- Businesses supporting the 'commuting office worker' lifestyle, such as coffee shops, sandwich bars, after-work pub venues, may have insufficient trade to make them viable.

- Public transport use is reported to be only between 30% and 60% of Before Corona levels. The business model of railways, tubes, and bus companies will change if commuting is reduced permanently by even just 20%. Certainly, urban and city services will lose substantial income.

- The fashion and clothing industries will change if huge numbers of people no longer buy smart suits, ties, shirts etc to maintain office-based business personas.

- Rural schools, once under threat of closure, may become oversubscribed and their limited facilities overrun. Meanwhile urban and city schools may flounder with fewer pupils, and even fewer teachers available to them.

For individual employees there could be a sting in the tail of showing that their work can be successfully completed without commuting to a central location. Once proven effective from Sussex, Somerset or South Ayrshire, it could also work from South Asia, where labour costs are lower.

Conclusion

This shifting of the working population from commuting to remote working, hints at significant impact on the status quo.

The current economic model has its roots in the industrial revolution, where people started to travel to work to use the latest manufacturing technology. This trend continued to enable employees to use (then expensive) information technology. Once people congregated in specific areas to work, other businesses sprang up around them to support both the people and the business. Stationery suppliers, printers, and sandwich bars, restaurants and convenience stores and many other businesses rely on the commuting model.

But information technology is now cheap and almost as mobile as the people using it, and the 2020 pandemic has shown that many do not need to commute in order to complete their work efficiently. How far the change from commuting to WFH will go and how permanent it will become cannot be predicted in the current volatile situation. It seems unlikely that the organisation of work will return completely to Before Corona patterns.

Peter Cheese, CEO of the Chartered Institute of Personnel and Development (CIPD) sees WFH largely as a good thing.

> "We now have a cultural shift that has been needed for a long time,' he says. 'Work was based on old paradigms and rules, such as presenteeism. The rigidness of the office culture may have held us back.
>
> … We know things are not just going to "snap back" to where they were before."

As the giant coronavirus experiment has shown that WFH is a possible, and sometimes the only, way for businesses to survive in challenging times, organisations are likely to at least adopt it as a continuity/disaster recovery strategy. They will hopefully be better prepared if a future situation requires it.

On the available evidence it seems that WFH is likely to increase more generally After Corona, and organisations and managers will view it more positively. But whether increased patterns of WFH will generate the changes to organisational culture and rewards required to make it effective long term, may depend on broader economic and political decisions.

Coronavirus has catapulted the evolution of WFH into a revolution. Its future may depend on how much organisations and government are determined to recreate the pre-coronavirus environment. In that scenario, transport systems and city centre businesses that support the commuting model, also survive.

An appreciation that this is an opportunity to embrace a new economic model, where work is not concentrated in some cities and some parts of the country, could have a positive outcome. There will be winners and losers. Those organisations that are agile and responsive to the changes could be winners. Those who don't or can't adapt to different business models, may not survive. If we ride out the upheaval of this revolutionary change, maybe we can move to a more equitable future that truly levels up.

Practical tips for developing your Working from Home strategy

1. Identify the benefits you want your WFH strategy to realise and for whom

2. Evaluate organisation culture for aspects of trust, open communication and business development

3. Adopt agile, responsive approaches to work practices and change management

4. Modify reward systems to prioritise achievement over input

5. Develop HR policies, IT systems and facilities management to support WFH

6. Involve all functions in decision making

7. Enhance managers' skills including ability to delegate work without needing to closely supervise

About the Author

Julie Huish

www.unitytransformation.com

Julie Huish, Director of Unity Transformation. started her career in Human Resources with a passion for Workforce and Organisational Development.

Through leadership roles, Julie gained a deep understanding of team cultures, barriers to change and the importance of staff engagement to deliver successful change programmes.

Julie's training as a Lean Six Sigma Black Belt enables her to teach Continuous Improvement Methodology and smart project management skills, enabling businesses to develop their own in-house capability to lead and manage change.

She is also a qualified NLP Performance Coach and Trainer to offer one-to-one support. Julie has supported a wide range of organisations from the NHS Acute and Primary Healthcare Providers to Private and Public Sector organisations in delivering successful change programmes.

70% of Change Programmes Fail – But Not on My Watch

By Julie Huish

Introduction

'Change' it's a funny old word. It comes in various shapes and forms such as Continuous Improvement, Change Management, Quality Improvement, and Transformation etc. and when implemented successfully, is 'Good for Business'.

When I started to write this chapter, my fellow CIPD Consultant and Peer, Marc Reid, asked me if I was including any statistics relating to change programmes.

To be honest with you, looking at statistics on the success or failure of change programmes wasn't something I felt the need to look at before.

I have always taken pride in delivering change programmes and projects for my clients that met their organisational goals.

In the last four years I have successfully facilitated 176 projects and programmes, coached leadership teams in how to lead and manage change and trained over 700 staff in Continuous Improvement Methodologies while developing a Culture of Continuous Improvement.

Imagine my shock when I read that 70% of change programmes failed.

Change management as it is traditionally applied is outdated. We know, for example, that 70 percent of change programs fail to achieve their goals, largely due to employee resistance and lack of management support[27]

As an HR Transformation Consultant and Lean Six Sigma Black Belt, I learned early in my career that understanding team cultures, barriers to change, and the importance of leadership and staff engagement was paramount to the delivery of successful change programmes.

But with so much focus on change in today's world, it's no wonder some of your staff are fearful and resist change.

In this chapter I will provide you with some tips on how to implement a sustainable improvement programme and minimise the risk of failure by using my Six Step approach.

Six Steps to Delivering Successful Change Programmes

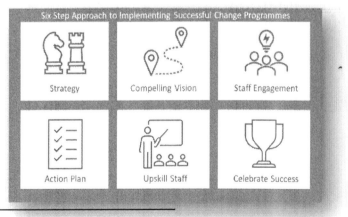

---

[27] Changing Change Management – McKinsey & Company, July 1, 2015

Why Change

There are many reasons why organisations identify the need for change. It could be Planned or Remedial Change, or reacting to external factors that have impacted businesses, such as the recent Covid-19 pandemic.

Most organisations know what areas need reviewing and/or improving within their business, but for some, implementing a sustainable improvement programme has proved challenging, causing disengagement across the workforce, and targets not being met.

For many years now I have been supporting businesses going through periods of change, and the main area that always requires a lot of focus is overcoming barriers to change.

I've listened to a lot of people talking about their fear of change, and whether it be fear of losing their job, fear of returning to work, or fear of losing their business, there is a strong overwhelming feeling of anguish towards change.

One conversation I heard was a man describing how great his business was doing last year – new clients, steady growth, and a real sense of achievement. His body language was positive, and his eyes lit up talking about his successes.

He went on to describe the impact of the Covid-19 pandemic over the last three months – furloughed staff, no revenue, lost business, and he ended his sentence with "I'm scared. I'm scared for my future, my business, and my staff".

His body language changed, he looked broken. As a small business owner myself, I could feel his heavy heart, and the stresses and strains weighing heavily on him.

As a Change Consultant, I wanted to reach out, but then his friend said, "Are you going to close down your business"?

The man replied "Oh no. I've been talking with my team and we've come up with some ideas on how we can get the business back on its feet".

"The way we offer our services will be slightly different, we have even come up with ideas for new products which we are branding and launching soon".

He continued, "It won't be easy, but we are confident it's the right thing to do".

He looked inspired and hopeful, and I could see a glimmer of light in his eyes.

In the space of 5-10 minutes he went through so many different emotions, highs, and lows, that finally ended with 'HOPE'.

He didn't need my help. He had a plan, a strategy, a compelling vision, and through talking to his staff and engaging them in the conversations about the future of their business, he had a culture of innovation and improvement.

With a little smile on my face and a gentle nod towards him, I knew he and his team would be ok.

Six Steps to Delivering Successful Change Programmes

When I work with organisations going through change, there are four key areas that I focus on. These are:

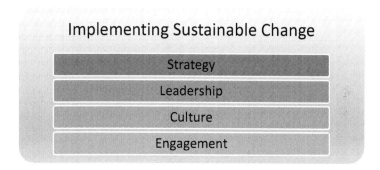

Remove any one of these elements and your change initiatives are likely to be unsustainable.

Within my six-step approach you will see that Strategy and Engagement have their own vital importance, however leadership of change, and embedding the right culture applies to all steps.

Below are my top tips:

Step One – Develop a Strategic Plan

Create a one-page Strategic Plan, detailing your vision and mission, what you want to change and the reason why. If you don't inform your employees of the 'why' there is a need for change, you won't have engagement.

Step Two – Create a Compelling Vision

 Within your Strategic Plan and Communications Strategy, write a compelling vision. A compelling vision is something that is meaningful, inspirational and of benefit to your staff.

Step Three – Engage your Staff

 Facilitate some Staff Engagement Sessions promoting two-way conversations, and actively listen to what your staff have to say. Take on board their comments and ideas and encourage them to get involved.

Step Four – Develop an Action Plan

 Following the feedback generated from your staff engagement sessions, create an Action Plan detailing all the ideas for improvement that have been identified, and ask for volunteers who would like to lead these mini projects.

Step Five – Train Staff in Continuous Improvement Tools

 Leading change projects does not have to be restricted to those in leadership positions. Upskill your staff in tools and techniques to lead and facilitate change, you never know what is around the corner.

Step Six – Celebrate Success

...... Even the little and quick wins

Star Tip:

In my experience the most successful change programmes have been sustained when staff of all grades, from frontline staff to leadership teams are actively engaged and involved in leading and facilitating change projects.

Break down your programme into bitesize chunks so you achieve results more quickly.

Reflecting back on the story above, I recognised that unwittingly this man had worked on the four key areas I focus on when helping organisations deliver their change programmes.

His approach:

Strategy:

He reviewed his products in line with his customer needs

Leadership:

He stood up to the challenges his company faced during the pandemic and embraced change with a new vision for the future

Culture:

He collaborated with his staff, inspiring a 'can do' attitude of innovation

Engagement:

He made joint decisions with his staff that benefited everyone

If you are facing challenges within your business, you too can identify and lead change yourself by using the six-step approach.

The next section of this chapter is a case study demonstrating how successful change can be achieved.

Case Study

I worked with one client who was undergoing a major transformation with regards to improving targets, meeting their customer demands, and complying with regulatory bodies.

As you can imagine, the scope of the programme was huge, but with a structured approach, strategic plan in place and training / coaching of staff complete, they not only achieved their goals, they embedded a Culture of Continuous Improvement that is still effective today.

Within six-months of receiving training in Continuous Improvement Methodologies, a cohort of 12 empowered staff successfully delivered over 50 improvement projects aligned to organisational goals.

How did the organisation achieve this?

By engaging staff at the start of their Continuous Improvement journey.

The leadership team knew they needed to improve their ways of working to meet the demands of the business, which included a move to 7-day working patterns.

This in itself was causing anxiety amongst the staff, however, they knew it was the right thing to do.

The leadership team created a one-page Strategic Plan defining the purpose of the change programme with a vision and mission designed to inspire and engage their staff.

The vision was compelling, it outlined the benefits to staff that were meaningful to them.

Through a series of communication events, they listened to their staff, and took into consideration all the What, If's and But's, and encouraged them to have a voice.

They knew their staff were invested in their organisation as they had an open, honest, and transparent culture. They knew if they tried to 'do change to them' the programme wouldn't work, so they empowered staff to make a difference.

What was their leadership style?

Their leadership style was supportive and based on trust and collaborative working. They operated a very flat structure rather than a hierarchical one.

Their focus was on coaching, supporting, and growing their people, empowering them to make decisions.

We facilitated innovation workshops to identify areas of improvement and generate new ideas for ways of working.

At the end of the session we created an Action Plan and asked staff of all grades, from admin support and junior staff to middle management supervisors, who would like to lead on some of the change initiatives.

How did they develop a Culture of Continuous Improvement?

By empowering staff to make a difference.

The staff who volunteered to lead on the change initiatives were provided training in Continuous Improvement Methodologies so they could lead and facilitate change in the workplace.

They created an Innovation Café showcasing the great work that had been achieved, with drop-in sessions for anyone who had an improvement idea and who needed support.

There was no top-down leadership approach, anyone and everyone had an equal opportunity to share their aspirations for growing and developing their business areas.

They celebrated their successes as a team, constantly reviewing and continuously improving through piloting projects until they were happy with the outcomes.

Their success was my success. That overwhelming feeling of job satisfaction when you see people and organisations achieve their goals.

In Summary

Change doesn't have to be difficult, it's your approach that defines your success.

There are many factors that need to be considered when implementing change, which is why some projects and programmes fail.

Have any of my projects failed? the honest answer is yes.

In my early career I was too focused on achieving organisational goals. Cutting costs or staffing and finding financial savings without considering the impact on staff, processes, and the quality of service to customers.

The lessons I learned was that the overarching key to implementing successful change projects is engaging, leading, and communicating with your staff at every step of your Continuous Improvement Journey.

Working together with your staff you overcome the barriers, enabling change programmes to promote Good Work and Good Business.

About the Author

Sally Stiegler

Sally has a passion for team and talent development and a deep curiosity for business, which inspired a career in Human Resources. She has held leadership roles with some fantastic global Companies, including Apple, Ermenegildo Zegna, and Coca-Cola. Shanghai was home to Sally and her family for 14 years, although her work spanned locations worldwide. With over 30 years of experience across multiple sectors, Sally is known for building trusted relationships across cultures, developing high performing teams, and her broad business acumen …. in addition to her laugh.

Sally's enthusiasm for team development comes from her sports background. Having long retired from playing competitive hockey, she now enjoys keeping fit, playing golf, skiing, and socialising with family and friends.

Culture Change - A Distraction or a Winning Strategy?

By Sally Stiegler

Over the years I have learned to carefully pick the moments I enter into conversations about culture, with leaders. The mention of "defining culture" has been met with rolling eyes and heavy sighs, understandable as it can seem a difficult, heavy topic. In response, I have been asked to draft descriptions of culture, which have been used in company communications to attract new employees, and worked with existing teams to draft culture "wish lists" hoping to create roadmaps to improve engagement levels and retention. On the positive side, these activities have raised awareness of cultural disconnects between leadership and employees and provided a starting point for meaningful conversations. However the work, often quite satisfying for the human resources team and employees involved, risks remaining "an HR thing" and having little business impact.

> *"Culture eats strategy for breakfast"*
> *Peter Drucker - Author, educator, consultant*

When striving to deliver the many challenges of leading an organisation successfully, the idea of spending valuable leadership time on refining or defining culture may seem a distraction, especially if the business is running relatively smoothly or already has a culture statement or list of values. Bear in mind though that company culture continuously changes, whether you work on it or not. It is shaped by the styles of new leaders to the team, often creating differences across departments and locations.

Culture needs to work in support of the business across the organisation. The late Peter Drucker, considered the father of "modern management", contested that regardless of how well-considered or solid a strategy may be **strategy will fail, or be significantly less effective, without a culture that supports the employees executing it.** Can your business afford to have a culture that does not fully support the execution of your strategies?

As with any strategic review, **it's essential to know when time will be well spent looking at your organisation culture.** Perhaps you find that what you're trying to get done is starting to bump up against the way the organisation operates, e.g. you need the business to work with speed while the team is intently focused on delivering as close to 100% perfection as possible. Or you recognise that a significant strategic change is required for the company to survive, which may also need a change in the way the organisation operates. You may be enjoying rapid expansion with a really high performing team, but are concerned that the organisation's speed of growth threatens the current culture. Expansion can put stresses on an organisation's culture, in particular to new markets, where new or local leadership styles and national cultures have a significant impact on the way things get done. These can be the critical moments to consider engaging in defining culture as a strategic tool that will support the execution of business strategy and enable the organisation to succeed.

Steve Jobs recognised that the culture he and his team had created was essential for Apple's success but was at risk as Apple's organisation expanded exponentially. In 2008 Apple University was established by Jobs to define the key behaviours underpinning the Apple culture and develop and implement global education programmes. Twelve years on, the culture at Apple has been significantly challenged by international expansion, but is largely enduring. Employees are taught about What Makes Apple, Apple, and why it is crucial for continued business success. At the same time, managers continue to be developed in the behaviours required to support and promote the Apple culture. For companies like Apple, culture has become a cornerstone of success. Defining the culture AND communicating clearly to employees the "why" behind the culture was a key to that success. Determining the "why we do things the way we do" strengthens our ability to develop organisation culture and gain full benefit of it's impact on the execution of strategy[28].

> *"Employee Engagement arises out of culture and not the other way around."*
> Carrick and Dunaway, Authors, Fit Matters

---

[28] Schorin & Wilberding; The X factor of great Corporate Cultures 2020

I have been fortunate to work with leaders who understand the value of defining and continuously developing company culture to create genuinely exceptional places to work. In locations or sectors that were experiencing shortages of talent, leaders were intently aware that enough elements of the culture needed to be suitably engaging to attract and retain talent with the qualities and skills that the business required. You don't need to have a culture that's attractive to all talent, just the talent you need[29]. And why be bothered with employee retention and engagement? Well, the value of creating exceptional places to work and retaining great talent reflects directly in business productivity. Gallup and other organisations which survey and measure employee perceptions have demonstrated that employee engagement consistently predicts positive business outcomes.

I find it worrying that employee engagement and business productivity were at all-time lows in the UK even before the Coronavarius crisis hit. Since 2012 Gallup has tracked a set of workplace metrics including employee engagement and the most recent data gathered in 2016 indicated a steep decline amongst employed Britons. Just 8% were found to be engaged at work, down from 17% in 2012. This was one of the lowest levels of engagement in Europe, higher only than Spain, Italy and France. Consider this in the context of UK productivity, which had not recovered since the 2008 financial crisis. The Royal Statistical Society calculated the average annual increase in productivity to be just 0.3%, compared to 2% a year, pre-financial crisis. At the end of 2019 UK productivity was more than 30% behind the US and 10-15% behind Germany.

---

[29] Erickson & Gratton; "What It Means To Work Here", 2007

Of course, there are several macroeconomic reasons behind the crisis in UK productivity, including significant economic instability, low levels of infrastructure investment and spending in research and development. We can however positively contribute to increasing UK productivity one workplace at a time, and, productivity within the workplace starts with employee engagement, which has company culture as its foundation.

Getting Started

There are many large consulting companies who are more than happy to provide their services to facilitate the development of your winning culture strategy. I firmly believe, however, that the answers lie within, with leadership and their teams best placed to define what is needed. It's helpful though to have a structure to follow to ensure time is well spent. And it doesn't have to be a massive project. As with any strategy development, a culture review can be included within a business planning process, or if you feel that you have hit a critical moment that requires some redirection of culture, introduce the subject as part of a leadership meeting agenda.

I have learned a lot about the development of culture, in different locations, working with Ermenegildo Zegna, Coca-Cola and Apple. Very different companies, serving different customer needs, with very different cultures; however, each share the same focus on culture as being a foundation for their success. The following Four-Step approach, which I have tried to bring to life through a real culture change experience, incorporates my learnings and provides a structure to think and plan for your culture strategy.

A Winning Culture Strategy In China

 1

Engage in Culture & Define a Vision

- *Review business strategies, competitive environment, talent needs and identify what is needed within the culture to be successful.*
- *Identify cultural elements from the past that will continue to serve the company well*
- **Define culture in terms of the critical FEW values, norms, beliefs, mindsets or behaviours**
- *Prioritise to a small number (3 - 10)*

I was involved in a particularly meaningful experience of developing organisation culture as a strategic tool while working for a leading Italian luxury company, Ermenegildo Zegna.

2006 was a critical year for Ermenegildo Zegna. Facing the potential for significant global growth, with pioneering footholds being created in new markets like China and Brazil, a new organisation model was created that could better support brand consistency and growth. This required a shift to being a brand and customer-led organisation from being organised around product categories. Leadership recognised that new behaviours would be necessary for the new model to work and for people to be able to operate successfully within the model. From this the "Zegna Mindsets" were born, a set of behaviours and principles defined by shareholders and leaders of the organisation which incorporated elements that

114

had delivered considerable success to the Company over the previous 90 years with new features considered essential to propel the Company forward. The Mindsets were communicated and activated by all teams around the world with the intent for everyone to:-

- *Understand the Zegna Mindset & why it was important for Zegna's future*
- *Know how it relates to them and their team*
- *Identify the behaviours they needed to work on to be successful*

A support kit was provided to each region that could be localised to engage their teams. The ability to localise was necessary as each location was at a different stage of organisational development, with substantial cultural variations reflecting regional cultural norms, in addition to having some fiercely independent local leaders. The Mindsets were integrated into the competency model used for development, recruitment and performance management.

At the time, I was working in Greater China with a relatively new and rapidly growing Zegna Retail team. It was a critical moment for the Greater China team to define and solidify a culture that would ultimately provide a foundation for remarkable business success in the Region. It was November 2008, the beginning of the global financial crisis that would see the survival of many luxury brands rely on the successful expansion and profitability of their businesses in Greater China and emerging Asian markets.

A number of the Mindsets resonated and enhanced the natural working style of the Greater China team; Inclusive, pragmatic and realistic, enthusiastic and positive. The team had these attributes in abundance. But Accountability, setting

High Standards and Targets and putting the Customer First were somewhat counter to the regional cultural norms often seen in Asia, particularly China. Workplaces in Asia have been found to emphasise "order through a cooperative, respectful and rule abiding culture", while "embodying caring and a sense of safety and planning"[30]. These were definitely cultural elements that were strongly present at the time, with harmony also high on the list. Speed of growth, geographical dispersion of the retail stores across the country and significant regional differences required local leadership to react appropriately to quickly changing situations. With these in mind we decided that developing a culture of Accountability and High Standards and Targets would be fundamental to achieving the growth potential of the market. Additionally, we recognised that these were important skills supporting a key talent strategy for developing local leadership.

Our leadership team also recognised that an additional element was missing which we believed would be fundamental to being successful as an authentic Italian luxury brand in China. We needed to bring some of the cultural elements synonymous with Italian life to the team e.g. sociability, food, drink, art and the feeling of being part of a broader Italian Zegna Family. And so began the fun of creating our high performing, unique, and highly engaging culture in Greater.

"In some ways clarifying a vision is easy. A more difficult challenge comes in facing current reality."

Peter Senge - Senior Lecturer MIT, Author, Systems Scientist

---

[30] Cheng and Groysberg; How Corporate Cultures Differ around the World 2020

2

Know Where You Are Now

- *Get input, feedback*
- *Go deeper to understand root cause of issues*
- *Honestly reflect with the leadership team*

Having identified the critical elements of culture we believed necessary for business success, and defined what we thought success would look like, we needed to be clear on where we were at that stage, and why that was. Culture is profoundly impacted by leadership style, decision making processes, and how we engage employees in change, so understanding our current reality required some significant leadership reflection.

It was imperative to elicit honest input from the broader team which, given the culture, we recognised may be challenging to get. Our Region Head was, however, adamant that collaboratively engaging and being open with the team would be fundamental to our ability to successfully develop the future culture of the organisation. This was step 1 of the change that had not yet been defined. Through mini-surveys and group discussions with trusted local leaders (not foreigners), we gathered the input that we needed to reflect more honestly on our current reality. We then went deeper with our teams. By facilitating root cause analysis sessions we

117

were able to more fully understand the key elements of current reality that needed to change.

The reality wasn't particularly pretty, in my experience, it rarely is, but also not surprising. We recognised that decision making and planning were purely in the hands of the leadership team, with the broader team waiting to be told what to do. The middle managers that head office communicated and worked with on a daily operational basis did not have the skills or confidence to push back on what they were asked to do. This lead to actions being taken that created issues for the China market and reinforced the tactic of middle managers towards self-protection and to decline accountability. Additionally team leaders saw little reason in having team meetings, as all actions and activities were communicated directly to individuals, and there was little team cohesion.

Starting with the leadership team, individuals and departments were doing their own thing. Team and cross-team sociability were pretty much non-existent. Not the Italian social environment we had in mind.

 3

Create A Tangible Plan

- *Identify areas of focus that will have the highest impact in supporting the change in culture*
- *Agree high leverage actions*
- *Put measurements in place*

With enough awareness of what was contributing to our current reality and increasing clarity on what success looked like, the building blocks for delivering our culture aspirations were defined, and an action plan developed. After creating an initial plan, progress was continuously reviewed, learnings captured, and actions revised. The chart below shows the key focus areas of our plan.

Leadership Team Development		
The foundation of the plan, based on "The 5 dysfunctions of a Team". A team journey to understand each other, value the impact of each department and the importance of collaborating across functions. Developed leadership and broader business skills, and increased performance expectations for all departments.		
Devolved Management	**Team Engagement & Communications**	**Organisation Development**
Developed skills of managers to lead and take accountability for cross function projects, and function plans. Implemented processes that challenged expectations & monitored standards.	Team engagement strategies based on "Organisation Capacity for Vision Creation" Provided opportunities for all employees to understand and contribute to business priorities & expectations. Sensibilities to Italian culture built through events, meetings & impactful moments.	Redefined the organisation to create 1 team ensuring consistent and high standards across the Region Developed clear department accountabilities Expanded the scope of management roles, retaining growing talent. Opportunities to up skill with new hires.
Measurement: Retention, Engagement, Training hours, Development moves Achievement of business plans and key business performance indicators		

Areas you may focus on	
Leadership style	Internal communications
Decision making	Performant management
Resource allocation	Rewards & recognition
Business planning	Competency models
Information systems	Succession planning
Reporting systems	Organisation development

 4

Communicate & Execute

- *Consider approaches to engage the team*
- *Consider level of commitment to the change needed by each group for success.*
- *Craft messages and reinforce in ALL communications*
- *Review and evolve the plan*

Team engagement and employee communications was a fundamental pillar of our plan. Where possible, we engaged the broader team in developing our ideas and actions to achieve maximum buy into the change. There were some aspects of the plan that were less appealing to specific parts of the organisation, particularly around organisation development. With strategy developed and agreed by leadership, we spent as much time as we could to create the execution plans with teams impacted by the change. At each stage we learned from the organisation, which allowed us to enhance our strategy.

Our work on culture development was not a one-off event. Neither was the work carried out in a vacuum. The culture strategy became an integral part of business activities, it had to, as we were redefining "the way things get done" for the business. As such, all business communications incorporated and reinforced messaging related to our culture change.

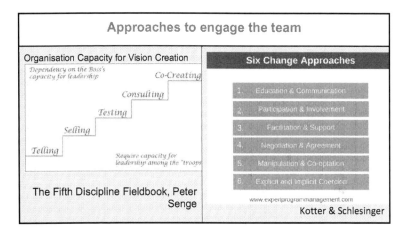

Results

Ermenegildo Zegna in Greater China became known for its unique culture and received the Fortune China, Employer of Choice Award, reflecting exceptional levels of employee engagement and retention. Developing the culture of

Accountability and High Standards & Expectations enabled the business to effectively expand across Greater China, develop an iconic fleet of flagship stores, implement winning business strategies and achieve exceptional results.

The Chinese consumer became ever more valuable to the Company and as they began to travel the world, our Chinese retail associates were deployed to the most visited European and US locations to support in accelerating their growth opportunities. It was the development in team sociability that was possibly the most satisfying aspect of the change. I knew that I was able to move on from my position when I attended an employee event with close to 100% participation of the Chinese team, and totally self directed in their socialising!!

The work of Patrick Lencioni and Peter Senge informed many of the approaches we took. I can highly recommend their books as reference material for any team or organisation learning and development.

> *"Teams that are immersed in a culture of accountability, collaboration, and initiative are more likely to believe that they can weather any storm"*
>
> *Rosabeth Moss Kanter - Professor Harvard Business School*

Now more than ever, we need our businesses to be highly productive and resilient. Consider if your business is at a critical moment of challenge, change or growth. It could be the right time to define a winning culture strategy that engages employees, supports your business strategies and drives business success. It's good work and good for business!

About the Author

Siân Perham BA (Hons) MCIPD

www.aligned-leadership.com

Sian Perham is a Leadership specialist, helping hundreds of leaders realise their leadership potential. Sian is skilled at creating safe environments to maximise people's learning opportunity. She is naturally collaborative, supportive yet challenging with a good sense of humour.

Sian runs Aligned Leadership, partnering with businesses to develop leaders who inspire others and get results.

Sian has been coaching and facilitating for over 15 years and is a Results Trained Coach with the NeuroLeadership Institute and a member of the CIPD. With extensive corporate experience, she has successfully facilitated and coached internationally; UK, China, Thailand, Philippines, Singapore, USA, Germany, France & Luxembourg.

How to take the difficult out of difficult conversations for greater performance

By Siân Perham

Introduction

There are certain conversations that people managers dread having, it might be about an individual's performance, addressing a specific behaviour, a project or meeting that went wrong, or discussing something that is particularly sensitive.

At the thought of a conversation, you feel anxious, nervous, frustration, anger, your palms are sweaty, your mouth is dry. On top of all that, you don't want to upset anyone, or be the bad person, or have the situation get out of control. There is a great temptation at this point, to question whether you can avoid the conversation altogether.

   Let me stop you right there!

Firstly, let me tell you this is absolutely normal.

Let me also say this is not a good reason to avoid the conversation. It is your role as a manager, it will benefit the individual, your credibility and the business, you should not avoid the conversation. This is a conversation that you need to have.

Having worked with hundreds of leaders on how to have difficult conversations there are four steps you too can take to transform a difficult conversation into one that is effective and impactful and gets you to the desired outcome, all whilst reducing your anxiety and stress level.

To demonstrate the use of the four steps, let me share Sam's experience.

Sam was promoted 12 months a go when the previous manager left. She's worked for the company for 3 years and has been identified as top talent. Since being promoted, Sam often feels overstretched and at times overwhelmed. She is doing the best she can, and sometimes wonders if that is enough. She needs to talk to Joe, a member of her team, about a meeting last week. Joe showed his anger and frustration in a client meeting and it's not the first time. The client emailed expressing their concern.

Until her promotion, Joe was her peer so she knows she should have had this conversation a while ago, but has been putting it off. She anticipates Joe will get angry and defensive if she tries to discuss it. On the back of the client email, she needs to do it sooner rather than later.

At the thought of it, Sam feels anxious and nervous.

What exactly is a difficult conversation you ask?

It's any conversation that when you think about it, triggers an emotional response in your brain. You might feel it in your stomach, you might sigh or hear yourself saying 'ughhh' (or something similar), you might even have an impulse to run away at that very moment – whatever your response, an emotional trigger and the physiological impact on us can be likened to taking the 5 year old version of our self into the discussion and it might play out something like...

Sam "Thanks for coming to the meeting and thanks for your time Joe. I want to talk to you about your behaviour in the client meeting earlier this week. Luke and Rory from Sales clearly pushed your buttons and you shouted, which is unacceptable with any client, but particularly this client as they are important to our business. Next time, I'd like you to make your point without shouting and upsetting that client. What do you think?"

Joe "Well, I didn't shout. If Rory & Luke from Sales had got their act together before the meeting then I wouldn't have had to say that is front of the client. Surely you agree the issue is with Sales, don't you?"

Sam "Well, I agree that Sales hadn't done what we'd asked them, but that's no excuse for your behaviour".

Joe "So, are you having a conversation with Luke and Rory then?"

Sam "I haven't no..."

Not quite the conversation that Sam had intended.

The 3 common pitfalls;

1. Emotions are driving the conversation
2. Sam becomes the 'parent' and the conversation sounds like a child being told off.
3. 0% accountability from Joe - not because he's a bad person. Joe is not being held accountable for his behaviour.

The likely outcome from this uncomfortable conversation is zero action, and a flicker of resentment, that longer term will get in the way of these two communicating effectively with one another. Relationships at work are a key factor in defining performance[31].

Difficult conversations are often about eliciting a different response, which means doing something differently. Let me introduce you to the 4 steps to take the difficult out of difficult conversations;

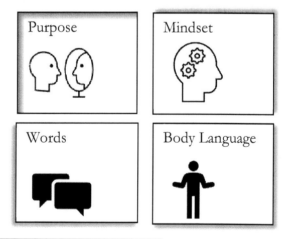

---

[31] (CIPD, Good Work Index Report 2020).

Step 1 - Purpose

Getting absolute clarity at this stage on the purpose and outcome of the conversation will make the other steps easier to navigate.

It's easy to fly into a conversation with an idea of the issue you want to address or feedback you want to give.

In Sam's example, the purpose is vague…

Sam knew that she needed to have a conversation with Joe about his behaviour in that client meeting and that he couldn't behave like that again.

So, if you need to address an issue that falls in your definition of being a difficult conversation, ask yourself the following questions and get 'super' specific with your answers.

What is the purpose of the conversation?		
X	**To give feedback** ✓	To explore the reasons behind the specific behaviour observed

Who is the conversation benefiting?		
X	I need….. I want…… I have to….. I should…. (starting with I is not the right motivation for a conversation ✓	For the individual, the team, the business, customers/clients

What is my expectation of the conversation and/or what is the specific outcome that I want to get from this conversation?		
X	That they accept what I am telling them and they have a plan ✓	That I am really clear in my message and I will open the meeting with that clarity

Had Sam got that clarity...

> *The purpose of the conversation is to explore the reasons for Joe's behaviour in the meeting The outcome is to address those reasons for the behaviour.*

Now apply this to your own reality and a difficult conversation that you need to have.

ACTIVITY

The purpose of the conversation I will have is

Who will benefit from the conversation?

Because

What is the ONE specific outcome I expect to get

The quality of the outcome is dependent on what you put in and difficult conversations are no exception.

Step 2 - Mindset

It is not uncommon to have played out the whole conversation in your head before you've even had it, so by the time you come to have the conversation for real it often plays out in two ways; 1) a 'tell' and b) a monologue.

The only guarantee I can offer if this is your chosen approach is that you will feel better.

Why? Because you will have got a lot off your chest and it's likely you ended the conversation along the lines of *"....and I think you should......[action]. Do you agree ?"*

Let's be honest, we've all done it. When you think about the outcome you want from the conversation, is there a better way to go about it. The answer is yes, absolutely!

Your time is a rare commodity and it's easy to fall into the trap of believing the quickest way to get someone to do something is to just tell them.

Hook of Accountability

Who needs to take accountability for the issue?

When we tell someone what to do about something, there is little or no accountability or engagement with the issue or indeed the outcome[32].

As was the opening monologue in Sam's conversation with Joe.....

> Sam *"Thanks for coming to the meeting and thanks for your time Joe. I want to talk to you about your behaviour in the meeting earlier in the week, when X clients came in and Luke and Rory from Sales were there as well. I think you raised your voice and that's unacceptable with any client, but particularly this client as they are important to our business. Next time, I'd like you to make your point without shouting and upsetting that client. What do you think?"*

The missed opportunity here is to hold Joe accountable for his behaviour.

---

[32] Leadership Continuum Theory. Tannenbaum & Schmidt, 1922

Let go of the need to be in control of the conversation

The greater the clarity and specificity you can bring to the purpose and outcome of the conversation, the more you can let go of the need to fix it with your solution.

Keep an open mind - It's easy to make assumptions about people. Sometimes we are right but mostly, we are not. We can't begin to know what drives other people's behaviour, what the root cause is, and what the action or outcome might be.

Less is More! Think about how you will open the conversation but don't script it any more than that….

ACTIVITY

Complete the sentence "What I want to talk to you about is

If it's more than one sentence, you are trying to fit too much into one dialogue. If you have more than one issue, identify which is the most important to address first?

Keep working on this until it's one sentence.

Begin the conversation from a place of curiosity and respect. Let go of the fix or solution to this problem. I

"The conversation is not about you"

acknowledge it's highly likely you've been there, done it, and have the T-shirt – but it's your fix.

There is no but…. In case that's what you've just said to yourself… it's not about you.

Step 3 - Words

"Listening is often the only thing needed to

help someone"

Iota of Truth

it's crucial to the conversation that you identify the facts. Facts can't be disputed whereas opinion can. In the case of Sam's discussion with Joe, the fact of the issue is that in the client meeting on that Monday, Joe raised his voice.

ACTIVITY

What are the facts of the situation?

Without the facts, opinion and judgement can creep in, the result of which is;

- You end up on the hook of accountability trying to justify your statements
- The other person is on the defensive and the message quickly gets lost in a war of words

---

Sam "I want to talk to you about the meeting on Monday. I thought you looked angry or frustrated in that meeting when you spoke about the customer implementation plan"

Joe "I wasn't angry, why did you think I was angry?"

Sam "Well, I thought you looked angry and you shouted at one point"

Joe "I didn't shout."

Sam "You did shout Joe, and I totally understand your frustration with the sales team. You really do need to control your anger in front of the clients"

Curiosity through Questions

"The art and science of asking questions is the source of all knowledge"

Thomas Berger

Curiosity is the ability to look beyond the obvious. To dig deeper.

Curiosity is an under-utilised skill. It's the difference between making assumptions and listening for what is really going on, which nine times out of ten will get you to a different outcome; here's how Sam achieved this…

Sam "Thanks for your time today and for coming to the meeting. I want to talk to you about the meeting on Monday. You raised your voice during the meeting and I am curious to understand what was going on for you that caused you to raise your voice?"

Jo "ughh, yes I did raise my voice you are right. I was a bit frustrated"

Sam "why were you frustrated?"

Jo "I know how important that client is and I was really relying on Luke and Rory to deliver the detailed proposal in time. It's not the first time that Luke has not delivered what I've asked him"

Sam "yes, I can understand and relate to your frustration. What impact do you think that had?"

Jo "I would imagine it made everyone feel uncomfortable"

Sam "Anything else?"

Questions get the other person to;

- Think for themselves
- Keeps them on the hook of accountability

Questions get you to the root cause quicker and the root cause is what needs to be worked on to change behaviour. Having got Joe to acknowledge the cause of the issue, watch what Sam does next to work towards a solution …

Sam "Okay, thank you for sharing that with me. So, this is not the first time that Luke has not delivered what he said he would deliver. I understand the frustration of that. What impact has that had on you?

Jo "I get really angry as I don't trust him"

Sam "Okay, so if you don't trust him, what can you do about that?"

Jo "Umm, well…. I could…… .

According to research by the Neuroleadership Institute, when someone feels a 70% ownership for an issue, they are 90% more likely to find a solution to it.

Step 4 - Body Language

"Body language speaks much more succinctly and honestly than mere spoken words"

Dixie Waters

Non verbal cues will often give away our real intention or thoughts without us even realising.

We know that Sam knew she needed to have a conversation with Joe, that she was nervous about Joe getting angry with her...

> *From the minute Joe got into the meeting, he knew that something was different. Sam looked very serious and stood up and shook his hand as he walked in. She had a note book in front of her and was clicking the pen. Her left foot was tapping the floor, which kept distracting Joe from what she was saying. She appeared to him to be nervous, which put him on edge as he wasn't sure what this meeting was really about.*
>
> *Joe is nervous and he can feel butterflies in his stomach. His palms are sweaty. He sits down and waits to hear what Sam has to say.*
>
> *He hopes his job is safe as he has just had an offer agreed on a new house, and he's just booked a holiday for the summer...*

Such is the power of our inner dialogue that Joe immediately senses something is up, so he starts to feel threatened. Is he going to be in the right frame of mind to have a constructive discussion? No!

I have seen managers have these conversations and the voice has great tone, speed, volume and inflection, but they are sitting with their legs crossed, one foot tapping on the floor, clicking a pen nib in and out, smiling (not Always appropriate), wrapping their arms around themselves, whilst looking anywhere apart from the other person in the face and looking like they want the ground to swallow them up.

Well, that might be a slight over-exaggeration, as I have never seen one person do all of those things at the same time, but I have seen the negative impact on trust and rapport when words and body language are mis-aligned. Without trust and rapport, the conversation is just a dance around the issue.

If we allow, emotions can take over and drive our body language and behaviour. Techniques such as meditation and breathing exercises can dampen down this emotional centre in our brain and ensure we approach the conversation using logic and rationale.

Set your intention for your non-verbal cues;

ACTIVITY

How do you want to appear;

Facial expression

Gestures

Eye Contact

Posture

The greater your awareness, the greater the impact you can have by managing your body language in the moment.

Summary

Imagine, you've just finished the difficult conversation that you were dreading.

You stated the facts, explored the issue with questioning curiosity, you listened and asked a few more questions. You were present, in the moment, felt calm and relaxed though out. Before you know it, you have the outcome you wanted and an individual who feels they have been listened to and is now keen to implement the solution you've help them identify. As a result, they feel empowered to deliver a great result and also comfortable that they can discuss issues and problems with you in the future without fear of judgement or blame.

That's what you call a win-win!

If you don't get it right first time, don't beat yourself up. Give as good as you've got and learn from your experience. The important thing is having a go, and doing something different.

You've got this!

Good luck!

Sián

About the Author

Marjory Mair BSc Hons; ACIPD; FRSA

www.mmairassociates.com

Marjory Mair Associates exist to help leaders and teams flourish and influencing their organisations for good. We believe that organisations are about people, so we work alongside CEO's and their teams, to develop new talent in order to stimulate growth and performance. We create environments where people are set free to think clearly and creatively and act courageously for their cause. We are passionate about, and role-model 'values-based' leadership that builds trust and engagement resulting in sustainable solutions for individuals, teams, organisations and society.

Marjory's approach to meetings encourages a collaborative approach particularly around issues that are often relegated to the 'too hard' box. As an executive and team coach, she loves equipping, creating and holding the space for leaders and teams to navigate complexity in problems and/or personalities to find solutions rather than become experts in the problem.

Making Meetings Marvellous

By Marjory Mair

"I wish I'd spent more time in meetings today" said nobody ever!

Marjory Mair

About Meetings

In my time, I've chaired and attended some jolly good meetings… and jolly bad ones. If I'm being honest, usually the bad ones I've chaired have been down to one thing … lack of preparation.

As a major communication channel to good work and good business, meetings can be a constant source of mystery, frustration and stress to business leaders. Yet we absolutely know that the conversation in a meeting directly links to the quality of decisions. We also know that the quality of these decisions lead to the buy-in to actions agreed and finally the quality of results.

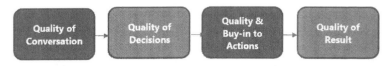

If we're serious about Good Work and Good Business, having Good Meetings is not a nice to have but a need to have. In fact, why stop at 'good' let's go for 'marvellous'.

Whether chairing, or participating, whether face to face or virtually, whether 1:1 or 1:100 here are some fundamental facts and principles to help you make your meetings marvellous.

The Cost of Broken Meetings

But first, why should we bother? Here are some rather surprising statistics about meetings:

- 13 days per year lost per person
- 56% of meetings are unproductive
- The cost to the UK economy is £45 billion
- The cost to small businesses £1m[33]

To cushion the blow of these painful statistics, here's some light relief in a cartoon that I came across in the meeting room of one of my clients:

---

[33] *The Independent, September 2018*

Meetings: The practical alternative to work. (via Ariel)

"So, what can we do about it?" I hear you ask.

Healthy Meetings

'Making Meetings Matter ' is one of my favourite workshops where I've helped over 2,000 people come to love meetings a little bit more, just because they realise they can control them a little bit more than they ever thought.

In these workshops, I ask people to think about a time when they attended a great meeting and then identify what was great about it and this list of features usually emerges:

- There was an agenda
- It was well chaired
- It started and finished on time
- Everyone participated
- There were clear actions
- People came prepared
- The food was good …

151

And we all know these things really do help, but they don't just happen and often they are not enough in themselves.

Broken Meetings

So, what gets in the way of having Marvellous Meetings? The question flips to identify things that stop meetings working well.

- People turn up late and we re-start the meeting every time
- There's no agenda
- We don't need to be there and the people who do, scnd apologies
- All the usual people do the talking just to look good
- We don't make any decisions
- There's no follow-up on actions so nothing ever improves
- People sit and do their emails or catchup on their social media
- The technology doesn't work and so much time is wasted

Ouch! Really . . . how often do we just put up with this stuff?

Whether face to face or virtual meetings, here are some top tips for you as the chair to make your Meetings Marvellous:

Top Ten Tips to Make Meetings Marvellous

1. Timing for the meeting

> "work expands to fit the time available"
> Parkinson's Law

Schedule the start at 5 past and finish at 5 to the hour … or even 10 past and 10 to the hour. Parkinson's Law states that "work expands to fit the time available" and we all know how a deadline focuses the mind.

Before virtual meetings became more common place we would allow ourselves time to move from our desk to a meeting room, now we get our physical exercise in moving between meetings by merely exercising the muscles in our fingers with a few mouse clicks hence little time for reflection. A few minutes to reflect after one meeting and focus before the next will stand everyone in good stead, not to mention the important opportunity to take a comfort break, have a good stretch, fill up our coffee cup, raid the biscuit tin …

2. Have a clear purpose

> "begin with the end in mind"
> Stephen Covey, Seven Habits of Highly Effective People

Engage the meeting members in the question: "What is the purpose for which this meeting exists?" This will create clarity on why we are having the meeting and focus on the outcomes and impact from the meeting rather than the inputs and the outputs. The impact of the answer to this question is in the interaction, sharing and crafting a clear purpose statement from which everything else about the meeting will be decided.

This clarity will give a clear indication on who should and should not be a core participant of the meeting and who may need to participate on an occasional basis.

This clarity will also avoid the trend towards what Patrick Lencioni calls "Meeting Stew" something I've noticed is particularly prevalent in times of high pressure and change.

3. *Be clear about behaviours that help achieve the purpose*

"clear is kind"
Brené Brown

For a regular meeting e.g. team meetings or project meetings, co-creating a set of ground-rules is a powerful way of engaging participants in a commitment to live out helpful behaviours in the meetings and allows them to hold each other to account for fulfilling the purpose of the meeting. In fact, I'd go so far as to say this is the most transformational tool I've experience, both in my own meetings and noticing what improves meeting effectiveness. When I was a team member a few years ago and my manager initiated this exercise after a meeting full of open conflict and tension, I remember a colleague, whom I had a lot of respect for, stating boldly "People should turn up on time because I think it's rude when they don't!". Well, guess who was often late for that meeting? Yes me! When that became one of our ground rules, guess who was never late again . . . yes, me! The power of these behaviours being created by the team meant I felt more ownership and accountability and the humiliation of being late to the meeting and labelled as 'rude' was not a label I wanted to wear.

A clear set of guidelines, principles, ground rules, whatever you want to call them keeps everyone safe and as Brené Brown says, "Clear is Kind."

4. Have a supportive agenda or a route map for the meeting

"if you aim for nothing, you'll hit it every time"
Anon

We all know it's helpful to have an Agenda for a meeting but in the pressure of everyday life it's not always easy. One organisation I know allows you to decline attendance at a meeting if the invitation isn't accompanied by an Agenda, even if it's your boss inviting you! Unsurprisingly, this results in a hastily produced list of four or five bullet points and seriously, I've noticed that they are as much use as a chocolate tea pot.

To make an Agenda really work for the meeting, let me introduce you to the idea of Nancy Kline, author of Time to Think and creator of The Ten Components of a Thinking Environment, who suggests the Agenda items should be couched as a question. So rather than an item headed "Budgets", replace it with a question such as "What are the critical factors we need to consider in next year's budget"? The beauty of this is that people can immediately start thinking about the critical factors rather than everyone bringing their own assumptions and opinions to the topic.

5. Engage everyone at the beginning of the meeting

> "leaders become great not because of their power,
> but their ability to empower others"
> John Maxwell

We all know it's easy to be physically present in a meeting but our mind is somewhere else completely – hopefully not reading emails under the pretence of reading the meeting papers! Moving swiftly on . . .

Start by inviting the participants to 'check-in' as a positive and engaging way to start the meeting. You can do this by introducing a question and inviting everyone to respond e.g. share one success in the last week or share one thing that you have learned since the last meeting. Give everyone a minute or two to think before anyone starts to speak and make it clear when to start sharing and the system for doing so e.g. round the room, call out names around your screen. The added benefit of doing this is that if some of the participants are nervous about speaking up, they have heard their voice early on and it's less daunting to speak the next time.

6. Encourage participation

"it never hurts to keep looking for sunshine."
Eeyore

When there is not enough participation and you feel like you are doing all the work and it's become a presentation or a webinar, don't struggle. Notice it, don't get grumpy or critical but craft a question and initiate 'Thinking Pairs' or Breakout Groups, where participants can engage with the question and come back to the whole group with some insights or ideas e.g. how can we make team meetings more interactive?

When participation is slow in virtual meetings or the same people are doing all the talking, step in and invite specific people to talk e.g. "Sam, what do you think?" Or if you want to hear from everyone, tell your participants and set up a system e.g. someone starts and chooses the next person, use alphabetical order, go round your screen and pop the sequence in the chat box so that people know who's next.

7. . . . but not all at once

> "you must extend to others what you want to receive
> - it starts with you"
> Susan Scott, Fierce Conversations

There is no doubt that rigorous dialogue is critical to creativity and problem solving however when there is too much or several people speaking at once, we limit the best solutions. I once watched a team member with the solution to a problem be talked over three times before she gave up. I'm so glad I was there that day to notice and ask her what she was thinking once everyone stopped talking.

When more than one person speaks at once or someone is dominating the meeting, set up a 'speaking system' e.g. round the room, or your screen, even alphabetical order, so that everyone gets the chance to speak. This has increasing importance in virtual meetings where you are less likely to notice subtle clues that someone wants to speak. I've also experienced the scenario where extroverts, who speak to think take up all the air space and the introverts, who think to speak don't offer their thoughts until two minutes before the end of the meeting – make space for them in the meeting. Again, this starts with a carefully crafted question followed by a clear 'speaking system'.

Encourage the meeting members to listen to each other rather than just wait for their turn to talk and your role at this point is to uphold the system – give clear eye contact to any interrupter, or virtually, call out their name. Tell them their turn will come then quickly revert to the person who was talking. Unless someone is about to die, stick to this system and continue another round until everyone has said all they need to say then watch how after two or three rounds the real question, decision or action emerges.

8. Turn it upside down

"let's end at the beginning ..."
Adaptation of quote from The Sound of Music

For formal meetings arrange Minutes of Previous Meeting and Matters arising at the end. This will drastically cut down the total time for your meeting by asking for amendments and matters arising to be addressed before the meeting. That will help production of the Agenda apart from anything else. Then cover off the Minutes of the last meeting and matters arising at the end of the meeting rather than the beginning – in one Trustee Group I've been part of, this has regularly shaved 45 minutes off the duration of the meeting.

9. Finish the meeting well

"catch them doing it right ..."

At the end of the meeting, invite the participants to share one thing that was good about the meeting or give appreciation to someone who has been particularly helpful in achieving the purpose or moving a tricky situation forward. Whilst this is a marvellous thing to do in itself, the added value is when you watch how it encourages the positive behaviour in future meetings. Adrian Wheatley has more to say about this in his Chapter "Working out how to lead – practical tips from an accidental leader".

10. When it all goes wrong . . .

> "nothing will work unless you do"
> Maya Angelou

It's strange how we always know when a meeting or part of it doesn't go particularly well or to be frank, goes badly. It's also strange how we can create a false sense of security around certain behaviours in meetings and tell ourselves "it wasn't that bad", or "if it happens again …" or "I'll probably just make things worse if I say anything"… or worse than that convince ourselves that it was "actually a good thing because …". Nancy Kline's wisdom once again encourages us to ask ourselves a few questions such as:

- What are you assuming that lets you ignore this?
- If you were to face it, what positive outcomes might result?

- If you knew that you can handle the fall out, what steps would you take to live free of this denial?

I find courage from Maya Angelou's quote that "nothing will work unless I do" and remind myself that this doesn't need to end up in a battle but rather a planned and respectful conversation with the individual or individuals involved.

For further help and practical tips on this, have a read of Sian Perham's Chapter on "Taking the Difficult out of Difficult Conversations."

11. If you do all that and it still doesn't improve ….

alt, control, delete

And here I quote from David Pearl's book on starting a business revolution one meeting at a time, which I'd highly recommend with the rather delicious title of "Will there be donuts"? His Tip No 5 suggests "If you can't improve a bad meeting … make it worse until even your most conservative colleagues realise things have to change." It'll come as no surprise that I always carry my knitting for this eventuality … only kidding!

So, because we've only got one life and we don't want to waste it or be the one saying "I wish I'd spent less time in meetings today". I promise that doing just one of these tips, will make your meetings better, and what's more, you might even enjoy them as well as achieve more – imagine that . . .

Good Work. Good Business. No Doubt. No question mark!

"Marvellous" I hear you say as you pick up or click your highlighter to choose your first tip . . .

About the Author

Marc Reid

www.mediation4.co.uk

Marc is an experienced workplace mediator, accredited by CEDR and Civil Mediation Council Registered. He has trained conflict management skills for many years and is author of '*DIY Mediation. The Conflict Resolution Toolkit for HR*' and '*8 Stages of Workplace Conflict*'.

Marc runs Mediation4 which helps organisations manage and resolve workplace conflict. He has mediated a wide range of cases and has also established and run mediation services for a top multinational company.

Marc combines his mediation expertise and knowledge with 25 years experience in senior corporate commercial, HR and general management roles. He also works as Board Director and Lead Mediator with the local community mediation charity and is an active CIPD volunteer.

Workplace conflict in a changing world – and how to deal with it

By Marc Reid

Introduction

Positive workplace relationships are at the heart of 'Good Work'. In the introduction to its 2019 UK Working Lives report[34] the CIPD sets out the principles of Good Work, including *"Good work provides a supportive environment with constructive relationships"*. A natural consequence of a positive working environment is good business outcomes. The CIPD Good Work Index 2020 report summarises this point well:

"Having strong relationships and teams are vital. It's hugely beneficial for our wellbeing (we notice their absence most when conflict rears its ugly head) and keeping work relationships productive goes hand in hand with high performance."[35]

Of course, the reverse is also true. Poor relationships are bad for those involved and have negative impact on the business.

---

[34] UK Working Lives – CIPD, 2019 p.3
[35] Good Work Index 2020 Summary Report - CIPD, 2020 p.5

One of the key challenges for businesses today is managing change. Change is happening at an ever-increasing rate[36] and represents a major risk factor for working relationships. The HSE identifies change as one of the six areas of work that can cause employee stress[37], and evidence shows that people experiencing stress are much less able to communicate effectively.[38] As any workplace mediator can confirm, communication breakdown is inevitably a key contributor to the deterioration of a working relationship.

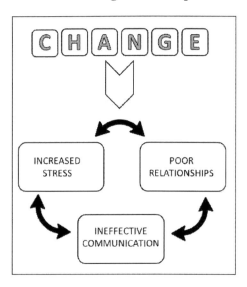

A recent example of rapid and fundamental change is that brought about by the pandemic. In this chapter I'll use the pandemic as an example of a business environment faced with significant change and resulting uncertainty. This type of

[36] Workplace Changes are Accelerating – Forbes, Feb 1, 2018
[37] How to tackle work-related stress – HSE, Oct 2009, p.3
[38] A Guide to Communication and Stress – Stress Management Society, 2017, p.2

situation heaps additional pressures onto workplace relationships generating substantial potential to escalate into employee conflict.

In the second half of the chapter I draw on my extensive experience as a workplace mediator to propose simple strategies to manage the danger of conflict and avoid escalation.

Jane had been dreading the day. She'd imagined she'd be relieved to be escaping the seemingly endless weeks of lockdown struggle, trying to home school her 2 children, manage all the cooking and housework as well as trying to look relatively decent for the endless Zoom calls that her work had become. But now her office was reopening and her team were being asked to return. Faced with the reality of trying to stay safe while getting to work and mixing with colleagues, plus all the existing stresses of delivering on her targets, she was not feeling at all resilient.

Pandemic and the impact of change

Jane's situation is one that many will have experienced in recent times as the gradual easing of the Covid-19 lockdown restrictions took place. Our whole way of life has been affected and this is certainly true for the workplace. Employees have encountered physical workplace changes such as revised seating arrangements, new work rotas and enhanced hygiene arrangements. More significant than these in my view are the mental challenges brought about by the change to the 'new normal'.

It was only lunchtime on her first day back and Jane was already nearing breaking point. She had nearly lost it on the train on the way in when a guy got on without a face covering and stood far too close to her. Her own handmade face mask, which had scared the children, was uncomfortable and she was glad to take it off when she finally got into the office. How the office had changed - screens up between all the desks, tape markings on the floor, hand sanitiser at every workstation. It was good to see the team again – well, except Martin. She'd never got on with him and during the team Zoom calls Martin always went on about how much he was enjoying lockdown – living in a lovely house with just his mum who looked after him like he was still 10. He had no empathy for how others like Jane might be struggling.

Employees have been nervous about returning to work – CIPD research in May 2020[39] suggested 4 in 10 were anxious about it. They return to a difficult environment and whilst many are glad to get back to something like a familiar routine, others could be overwhelmed by a host of concerns – their experiences during lockdown, worry about their personal safety, financial concerns, personal loss, job security and

[39] '4 in 10 people anxious about returning to the workplace as government prepares to publish guidance' – Press Release – CIPD, 9 May, 2020

anxiety caused by the massive changes in society generally. Environments like this, riddled with change, uncertainty and fear, are fertile breeding grounds for employee conflict. There is significant potential for minor niggles between employees to fester and escalate into major disputes. This is especially the case if you bring together people who have had differing experiences – how for instance do people who have continued working, often at risk to their own safety, view colleagues who have been furloughed and not been at work?

By the third day back Jane had thought things were getting better. She'd arranged to come in later which meant the train was empty enough to maintain social distancing and it gave her time to sort out the rest of the family before leaving for work. She'd been feeling more comfortable – until the team meeting. Before their manager arrived Martin was telling anyone who wanted to listen how he had repeatedly broken the lockdown, going out to see friends and having lockdown parties. Jane's sister was a nurse so she

found Martin's attitude outrageous but she knew that saying so would get her nowhere. So she held her tongue – until Jennie, the manager, asked Martin whether the report was finished and he said everyone had input apart from Jane. That was it, she'd had enough and called him something her mother would not have approved of. Of course it was wrong in front of the whole team, but she'd explained to Martin yesterday why she'd been late with her input and it was a genuine reason. There was no need to throw her under a bus in front of the boss. Martin's response was to call her childish and unprofessional in a way which sounded incredibly condescending to Jane. Jennie brought the meeting to a rapid conclusion and asked to see them both the next day.

The pandemic is an extraordinary event and hopefully we are unlikely to see anything similar in the near future. But what it represents is not unusual at all. It is an event which has caused significant change and disruption both in our personal and workplace lives. Change and disruption will not go away once the current crisis is over. It was present before Covid-19 arrived, for instance the increasing use of automation and the rise of the gig culture, and it will undoubtedly remain after the pandemic. So being able to manage the impact of these disruptions and the potential conflict that can result are critical skills to have.

> *"Change and disruption will not go away once the current crisis is over... being able to manage the impact of these disruptions and the potential conflict that can result are critical skills to have."*

Over the course of my many years as a workplace mediator I have seen the painful consequences of relatively minor issues escalating into major conflicts, as the situation has not been addressed early. How do we avoid the potential escalation of workplace tensions and the resulting unnecessary conflict?

Here are five strategies that employees can apply to help prevent conflict arising and when it does arise, help nip it in the bud before it becomes serious.

Strategies to prevent and handle conflict

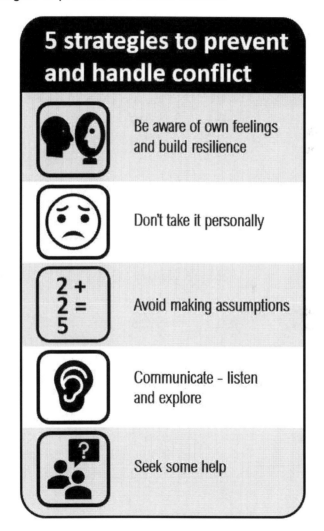

5 strategies to prevent and handle conflict

Be aware of own feelings and build resilience

Don't take it personally

Avoid making assumptions

Communicate - listen and explore

Seek some help

1. Be aware of own feelings and build resilience

 You know how people ask 'how are you' but are not really interested in the answer? Try this on yourself but take good note of the answer. Are you feeling strong and confident or are you not feeling great at the moment and a bit fragile? You could even rate yourself 1-10 and if you are towards the lower end then be aware that you are more at risk and avoid situations that could trigger you. And if you are triggered despite this, then remind yourself that you are not in the best state to deal with it and don't react or respond until you have had a chance to reflect. You can also work on your resilience by avoiding negative self talk and doing things which help boost your state of mind such as physical exercise and mindfulness practice.

2. Don't take it personally

 When someone is negative towards you it can feel very personal and hurtful. But often their behaviour is the outcome of what is going on for them as opposed to something which you have caused. For whatever reason you have become the focus of the negative behaviour their personal situation has created. For instance, perhaps their partner is giving them a tough time and it's easier to take out their frustration on you rather than on their partner. So try not to take it personally. This may be enough to help you let the negative feelings go, but if not, you will

need to address the situation rather than let it eat away at you and cause stress.

3. Avoid making assumptions

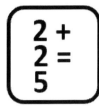

Our natural inclination is to try to make sense of experiences we have. If something happens which seems strange or unexpected the brain will try to fill in the gaps, to build a story of what is going on. We begin to make assumptions based on the information we

have to hand. This information may be quite limited so we look back for other situations that can help build the story. Let's say you are part of a project team and the team administrator organises a meeting but doesn't invite you. You will start to wonder why you haven't been invited. You might recall overhearing the team administrator mentioning your name when they were talking to another team member yesterday. You will start to make assumptions, to fill in the gaps of missing information. Perhaps it was a mistake you were left out, or was it on purpose? Do they not want you at the meeting? Why not? Does the team administrator have a problem with you or are they acting on instructions from the project manager? You can very quickly go down a path which leads to some uncomfortable conclusions and potential conflict with the administrator or manager. But this is all based on assumptions. Check what assumptions you are making and try to come up with alternative options – in particular options which assume less negative intentions. Ideally, don't rely on assumptions but instead check them out by talking to the person who can then explain.

4. Communicate - listen and explore

Every mediation agreement I have ever written includes a section on how the participants are going to communicate going forward. When a relationship breaks down communication deteriorates and as communication worsens, so the relationship suffers even more and so on until there is a major breakdown in the relationship. So if you are struggling in a relationship with someone, difficult as it may feel, it is really important to have a conversation with them about it. Try to approach it with an open mind and be willing to hear how they see things. Explain that you are concerned for the future of the relationship and that you want it to improve and want to discuss with them how that can be achieved. Explain to them briefly how you see things, using neutral, non blaming language and then listen to what they have to say. Try then to explore options and solutions which will work for both of you to make the situation better, in particular focusing on how you both want to communicate going forward. It can feel really challenging to even attempt this kind of conversation but if it means you can stop the pain and suffering this relationship is causing then it will be worth it.

5. Seek some help

You may find that you've done what you are supposed to do but it's still not resolved. You've tried to be resilient and have resisted taking it personally; you even had a conversation with the other person but despite both of you making an effort it is still a problem and you can't see a way forward. Don't be hard on yourself, this can happen. You now need to take the next step which is to seek help. This will probably be your line manager in the first instance – unless it is your line manager who you have an issue with, in which case it might be HR or your manager's manager. Whoever it is they might be able to facilitate a conversation between you and the other person. Or, if they feel they need some independent support, they can turn to a mediator. Some companies have trained employees who can help out in these situations, or you can access external help by turning to a professional workplace mediator. They can help you and the other person talk through the situation, understand where the issues are, explore what you need from each other and help you to come to agreement on how you will work together going forward.

Jane had been feeling really nervous about meeting Jennie the day after the team meeting incident. She knew she'd been out of order but she'd been provoked and on top of everything else it had been the last straw. Luckily Jennie really listened to her and it was such a relief just to talk about it to someone. Of course Jennie couldn't condone

175

what Jane had said but she did recognise it was out of character. Jennie suggested that they get together with Martin in a couple of days to talk things through. That hardly felt comfortable for Jane. Really she wanted Jennie to say that she'd speak to Martin about his behaviour but Jennie made it clear she wanted them to address it with each other. The meeting took place a few days later and started awkwardly, Martin wouldn't even look at Jane. But he wasn't angry and aggressive as she'd feared so Jane said what she was feeling, which was that she felt bad for swearing at Martin, acknowledging it was wrong. This seemed to trigger something in Martin and he opened up, explaining that he comes across as all confident and cocky but actually he'd been having a really difficult time during lockdown and he'd had no-one who he could talk to about it. His way of dealing with it was to pretend everything was fine. He really hadn't intended to 'drop Jane in it' in front of Jennie, he just hadn't stopped to think what impact his words might have. They both recognised that the wider issues had affected the relationship and agreed they would be more considerate of each other when they were interacting. It was a big relief for Jane — at least that was one thing less for her to worry about. Now, what did she have at home she could cook for dinner without having to queue at the supermarket...?

About the author

Julie Taylor

https://www.gardner-leader.co.uk/specialist/julie-taylor/

Julie Taylor is a specialist employment solicitor and Partner at Gardner Leader LLP in Newbury. She has over 13 years' experience advising both employees and employers on all aspects of employment law. She is always keen to ensure that all recommendations reflect the practical realties of the particular situation. She has often been quoted in the media, such as Personnel Today and Moneywise and is listed in the 2020 Legal 500 rankings as a Recommended Lawyer for Employment Law, where she was noted for consistently providing "expert, pragmatic advice" and an "excellent, responsive service".

What about Employment Contracts?

By Julie Taylor

The Employment Contract

In implementing any recommendations to improve working practices, employee relationships, or at times of significant change for your workforce, it is important not to overlook the basis of that relationship: the employment contract.

Having a clear, easy to understand document setting out the expectations and obligations of each party is vital, not least to comply with the minimum requirements of the Employment Rights Act but also to understand the boundaries for making changes and help avoid costly employment disputes. In addition, it is an opportunity to introduce new employees to your business style and ethos.

This chapter will provide you with an understanding of the key components of the employment contract and highlight some key issues to be aware of if you wish to change the

179

terms of the contract and some employment law basics. It is not a substitute for legal advice!

The Employment Rights Act 1996

The requirements of this legislation must be met by all employers and section 1 deals specifically with the details that must be provided in an employment contract or written document. This has been added to over time and significantly since 6 April 2020 all employees and workers have been entitled to a written contract setting out certain specific details from the first day of their employment.

This statement of initial employment particulars that must be prepared for everyone who works for you has to include the following details by law:

(a) the names of the employer and worker;

(b) the dates when the employment began and when any continuous employment started;

(c) details about pay, including frequency and rates;

(d) details of the hours required, including:

    i)   the normal working hours,

    ii)   the days of the week the worker is required to work, whether or not these may be variable, and if so how they vary;

(e) holiday entitlement, including pay, pubic holidays and calculation on termination of employment.

(f) arrangements in the event of sickness or injury and details of any sick pay;

(g) any other paid leave entitlements;

(h) pension entitlement and any other benefits;

(i) the length of notice required or duration of the contract if it is not a permanent position;

(j) job title or description of work;

(k) details of any probationary period;

(l) the place of work;

(m) whether any collective agreements apply;

(n) whether any work outside the UK is required (and further details if so);

(o) any training entitlements or requirements;

(p) the disciplinary rules applicable or details of where this information can be found; and

(q) Details of how an appeal or grievance can be raised.

Other terms to consider

The legal requirements focus on transparency for the employee so that they can clearly understand the terms that they have been offered to work under and how they will be paid for their work. This transparency is an important basis for a good working relationship.

However, employers will usually want to consider a number of additional terms in the contracts to help them keep control of their workforce and ensure that they have a contractual remedy should any dispute arise. It is also important to consider what flexibility might be required to adapt in times of significant change and how the contract can support this. These additional terms often include the following:

1) Confidentiality
2) Data Protection
3) Warranties

4) Restrictive covenants
5) Compliance with other policies
6) Lay-off & short time working

Confidentiality

While employees are working for you there is a limited term implied into the employment contract that they will keep your confidential business information secret and slightly more protection for specific "trade secrets", however, it will always be preferable to take steps to protect your confidential information in explicit terms of the employment contract. Where a business is evolving, it will also be important to ensure that the definition provides some flexibility.

Faccenda Chicken Ltd v Fowler [1987] Ch 117).

Trade Secrets has a limited scope and examples given by the Court of Appeal were identified as: secret manufacturing processes, designs or information with a *"sufficiently high degree of confidentiality" and all the circumstances will be relevant.*

Data Protection

It is vital to have an awareness of the General Data Protection Regulations[40], both in how you handle your employees' information and in how they are handling information belonging to your customers.

Previously it was typical to include provision in the employment contract for the employee's to consent to the handling of their information, but you now need a specific

---

[40] General Data Protection Regulations 2016

privacy notice reflecting the seven principles[41] to protect individuals' data.

Warranties

There are two key warranties or legal promises that are generally worth including the contract. The first relates to the employees' immigration status and would seek to provide confirmation that the employee is eligible to work in the UK and therefore take up the employment, although this would not displace the employer's primary responsibility for verifying their status.

Secondly, a warranty that the employee will not breach any other contract by entering into the terms of your employment contract is useful as it should highlight whether the employee has any restrictive covenants in their contract with their previous employer.

Restrictive Covenants

Wanting to limit competition and restrict what ex-employees can do when they leave a business is often top of the list of requirements, however, including such clauses comes with a health warning that they may not be enforceable if challenged and the court considers them to be an unreasonable restraint of trade. However, where there are legitimate business interests to protect, and the clauses do no more than reasonably necessary to protect these interests, then there are plenty of examples of the restrictions being enforced.

---

[41] Lawfulness, fairness and transparency, purpose limitation, Data minimisation; Accuracy, Storage limitation, security & accountability.

One of the real benefits for employers is that the cost of having a legal dispute about breach of covenants is huge and therefore often simply having restrictions included (provided they are still reasonable) can be a significant deterrent and therefore still provide some protection for the business, but they do need to be reviewed regularly to ensure that promotions, for example, or other changes are taken into account.

Compliance with other policies

It is also common to include express obligations in the contract that the employee will comply with the employer's handbook or other specific policies.

Lay-off & short time working

These clauses are very unpopular with employees and you will need to consider carefully whether you wish to incorporate such provisions, weighing up the competing interests, but they can be useful for industries where workloads fluctuate to help them cope with changes in demand. The clauses seek to reserve the contractual right for the employer to use short periods of lay off or shorter working periods in times of reduced work to reduce their salary expenses. Without this contractual right, imposing reduced working would be a breach of contract unless the employee specifically agreed or if there was a relevant trade union agreement. The clauses are intended to avoid immediate redundancies where work will return to previous levels within a short-period of time. They will also be drafted to fit with the statutory guarantee payments scheme. Employees placed on short-time working or periods of lay-off retain the right to request a statutory redundancy payment if the period if the arrangements continue for 4-6 weeks in a 13 week period.

In recent times we have seen the introduction of the furlough scheme, which was essentially a much more generous version of these provisions, but given the special circumstances the scheme was implemented to address and the cost, it may have a short lifespan.

Employee handbook

Employee handbooks can cover a wide variety of issues, such as dress codes and expenses to ethics and equality. Some will be important to assist with defending any claims from employees to show that the employer had taken reasonable steps to prevent the activity complained about (harassment, for example), although this should be supplemented by regular training. Others will simply deal with the practical mechanics, such as how a performance issue will be addressed. They are also useful to demonstrate again the business' culture.

Generally the handbook will be contained in a document quite separate to the contract to seek to avoid creating additional contractual obligations.

Changing the terms of an employment contract

Providing a new employee with a contract is quite straight forward and whether any negotiation on the terms follows at the start of the relationship depends on the objectives of the particular individual and the particular circumstances.

However, how do you vary the terms of your existing employees if a change in circumstances requires a new working pattern, for example?

Changing an employment contract follows ordinary contract law principles and therefore the contract can only be changed in specific ways, either:

i)   In accordance with its terms;
ii)   By agreement between the parties; or
iii)   By the unilateral imposition of a change that the other party does not object to.

Flexibility clauses

It is common for certain clauses in the employment contract to specifically reserve the right for changes to be made, such as to the location of the office or the scope of the employees' duties.

However, while this does provide an easy way to highlight and discuss the changes the employer wishes to make, the employment tribunals have highlighted that rights of this nature still need to be exercised reasonably and therefore the ability to rely on these provisions is limited.

By agreement

To achieve certainty that the updated terms have been agreed, the best method is to seek the employees express agreement to them, either by signing a new contract or providing a side letter setting out the details. Before setting out to agree changes with your workforce, it will be important for the employer to consider the business case for requiring the variation. The likelihood of reaching an amicable agreement to the new terms will increase significantly if there is good communication about the reasons why the new terms are required, which is even more vital in a period of change. Sometimes this will be unpopular, for example, where the terms of contracts are being standardised and terms are perceived as less favourable.

Therefore, the employer may be reassured to know that it can become an option for them to serve notice on the existing terms and offer employment on the new terms if agreement cannot be reached.

If the employee still does not agree, their employment would terminate on the expiry of the notice period and whether they have an unfair dismissal claim will depend on the reasonableness of the need to make the change, the changes themselves and how the consultation has been conducted. If 20 or more employees could be dismissed as a result, then specific collective consultation rules will apply.

Unilateral changes

This is probably much more common than the label suggests as many pay rises are implemented on this basis and the change is incorporated because employees are typically very happy to accept a higher salary!

Be careful in a situation where an employee objects to a specific change as this would not then become part of their contractual terms unless a specific agreement is subsequently reached.

In addition, if this is used for changes that the employee considers is to their detriment, then there is a risk that they could resign and bring a constructive unfair dismissal claim based on a breach of trust and confidence.

Top tips for changing terms

Step 1:	Consider the business case for requiring changes.
Step 2:	Carefully consider whether the change is permitted by the contract or not and draft the new clause.
Step 3:	Propose the new clause to the employees and the reasons why to seek their agreement. This would involve offering to meet to discuss any concerns.
Step 4:	Consider all concerns raised and make any amendments to the new clause that can be agreed.
Step 5:	Issue new terms for signature and ensure a list is retained to ensure all new contracts are returned.
Remember: if more than 20 employees are affected additional rules apply and it is only once full consultation has been carried out that it may be possible to serve notice and offer employment on the new terms. Specific legal advice is recommended.	

Employee rights

As an employer, it is also vital to have an awareness of the specific legislation designed to promote and protect employee rights in the workplace. These are numerous, but the following are good starting points:

    i)   The Equality Act 2010

All employees are protected from discrimination before their employment starts through the recruitment processes. There are nine protected characteristics and employees must not be treated less favourably or be subjected to harassment because they have or are associated with anyone who has one of the characteristics. Consequences of a discrimination claim can be severe with no cap on the amount of compensation a tribunal can award as well as the associated bad publicity.

> **Protected Characteristics**
>
> Age.
> Disability.
> Gender reassignment.
> Marriage and civil partnership.
> Pregnancy and maternity.
> Race.
> Religion or belief.
> Sex.
> Sexual orientation.

ii) The Employment Rights Act 1996

As well as setting out the requirements for the employment contract, this legislation also provides the protection from unfair dismissal and rights to redundancy payments.

Terminating an employment contract should be undertaken with care and legal advice is recommended, but it is useful to be aware of the five statutory reasons that can be a fair reason to terminate a contract. These are: Conduct, Capability, Redundancy, Illegality and Some Other Substantial Reason. Each have their own processes and procedural requirements to ensure that the end dismissal is fair and the key will always be to discuss with the employee to find out all the facts and consider all alternatives before making the final decision.

Employment law action points

Employers should regularly review their contractual documents and handbook in any event, but these are some tips to help with compliance overall:

Create an anniversary date to review your contractual documents every year. As many employment changes are announced in early April, that may be a good time or perhaps to coincide with the financial year of your business.

In your review, consider the following:

    a. Are they clear and easy to read?
    b. Are the legal requirements met?
    c. Are any changes required?
    d. Are the contracts consistent across your team?
    e. Are any new policies required due to changing circumstances or legislation?

Conclusion

So employment law will be with you every step of the way as your business grows its headcount or in changing circumstances, but rather than view it as a mountain of red tape or additional burden, simply consider that the rules and regulations are there to help ensure business owners treat staff as they themselves would like to be treated; reasonably, fairly and consistently with others.

Good communication is also an excellent way to avoid disputes and misunderstandings and will be crucial in agreeing changes to the underlying employment contract.

Printed in Poland
by Amazon Fulfillment
Poland Sp. z o.o., Wrocław